GLOBAL INNOVATION

GLOBAL INNOVATION

Edited by Jonathan Reuvid

University of Buckingham Press

University of Buckingham Press, 51 Gower Street, London, WC1E 6HJ
info@unibuckinghampress.com I www.unibuckinghampress.com

Contents © Jonathan Reuvid
The right of the above author to be identified as the author of this work has been asserted in accordance with the Copyright, Designs and Patents Act 1988. British Library Cataloguing in Publication Data available.

Print: 9781787198609
Ebook: 9781787198593
Set in Times. Printing managed by Jellyfish Solutions Ltd
Cover design by Simon Levy I www.simonlevyassociates.co.uk

Global Innovation

Editor: Jonathan Reuvid, University of Buckingham Press

FOREWORD

Global Innovation comes at an interesting time for UK industry. Companies all over the world are facing two unavoidable challenges; climate change and digitisation. Both are disrupting the way we trade; whether that is how global value chains or business processes operate or how companies interact with customers.

What is a certainty is that innovation will be critical in finding sustainable solutions to the issues we all face. Those companies that can adapt and respond with new solutions to the everchanging world around us will be those more likely to succeed, just like those companies trading into international markets will be more resilient than those that don't.

At the same time, the UK is about to embark on the largest upheaval of trade relations in over a generation, which will quite likely last a generation before the process is finished. Where the UK will be at the end of the process is hard to predict, except to say it won't be where the country is today. The UK is leaving the EU at a time when power and size are increasingly the levers being used to exert influence on the trading system, and the UK is going it alone when other countries are busy strengthening ties with neighbouring countries and regional trade blocs.

There will be no room for past grandeur or overinflated sense of privilege. The UK will need to be pragmatic and agile whilst playing to strengths in order to find new ways to work in partnership to really capitalise on the opportunities. The ability to innovate and reinvent itself is at the heart of what makes the UK so successful as a country and often what sets UK industry apart from most of the rest of the world. This book provides a timely toolkit that combines everything you need to know about how to promote innovation with a helpful framework on how to trade and where some of the opportunities are.

There has never been a more important time to be well informed on trade. If there is one thing, we have all learnt over the last three years of public debate, it is how little we know about trade and how much we take for granted. That is clearly not a sustainable position. Today trade touches every walk of life, and if we are to deliver global solutions to the big challenges of the day like climate change and digitisation we need to be working side by side with the developing world to stand any chance of long-term success. If there is one country in the world right now, with the right skills, networks and resources to play a major role in the task ahead, it is the UK.

Chris Southworth
Secretary General, ICC United Kingdom

INTRODUCTION

Global Innovation is a call to arms for British exporters of goods as the UK enters a pivotal period of resetting its international trading relations post-Brexit. Whatever the outcome of the current negotiations on trading terms with the EU, the challenges are considerable and need to be viewed against the changing status of the UK as a global exporter and importer over the last 20 years.

In 1999 the value of UK goods exported was $267 billion and of goods imported $310 billion, with a trade gap of $43 billion. The UK ranked 5 in both world exports and imports behind the US, Germany, Japan and France. In 2018 the UK exported $482 billion against $674 billion of imported merchandise; the trade gap had widened to $192 billion. Thankfully, the UK has maintained its healthy surplus in services trade, reported at £104.6 billion in 2018 and reducing the net trade deficit in sterling to £47.8 billion. More seriously, as a global exporter of merchandise, the UK's ranking has slipped to 10 while maintaining its status as an importer at 5. In exports China now ranks first before the US, with the Netherlands, South Korea, Hong Kong and Italy also outperforming the UK. The value of Germany's merchandise exports, in third place, is now 3.2 times that of the UK (2.3 times in 1999).

Three factors contributing to this decline are: the reduction in the UK's competitive manufacturing sector, the rise in low-cost manufactures from Asia and, since 2016, an element of inertia generated by the uncertainties of exiting from the EU into the unknown. Established exporters and those embarking on export need to be aware of the problems and plan how to address the opportunities.

Instead of focusing on those markets only where the UK has been most successful, exporters now need to broaden the list of priority targets to include high-growth import markets where they have less or minimal traction. This book contends that the key to successful exporting is innovative offerings which supplement the traditional solid attractions of high quality, excellent delivery and after-sales service, and competitive pricing and payment terms. Innovation in research, processes and end-products has long been a UK strength and can be marketed more aggressively with government support.

PART ONE

The first of the book's three parts is devoted to innovation and contains chapters highlighting the benefits of partnering with research establishments and universities to generate innovative offerings with contributions from Harwell Science and Innovation Campus and Coventry University.

An article from Basck emphasises the importance of a strong brand strategy and is supplemented by chapters from Olaf Swanzy identifying the grant funding that may be available for UK companies and from May Figures and RandDTax identifying the tax allowances and rebates that may be available for research and development and how they may be claimed.

PART TWO

Turning to the fundamentals of export trading, the second part of the book, intended as a primer for the less experienced and new exporter, opens with a chapter from patentGate emphasising the necessary actions for maintaining patent integrity in advance of market entry followed by advice from BExA on how best SMEs may start out as exporters.

Further chapters discuss the merits of connecting with Chambers of Commerce and other enablers via the Taio IT platform to break down barriers and provide briefings on the critical features of Incoterms, export credit and banking.

For many UK companies, their exports derive from their position in an international supply chain, and a further chapter from CIPS indicates the shape of things to come in procurement and supply.

PART THREE

Research into the most promising market opportunities for exporters starts with an appreciation of how the WTO regulates world trade and where the UK could stand after conclusion of its trade deal with the EU. Moving on to identification of priority markets, developing a strategy for enhancing exports into established territories and establishing footholds in unfamiliar markets where the UK presence is weak, the next chapter pinpoints the standing of leading British product groups in comparison with its competitors.

A shortlist of 15 priority markets is established where the greatest opportunities for nurturing existing exports lie. In the Appendix that follows the import patterns of each of the 15 countries is analysed in tabular form, again identifying the relative success of the UK's major competitors in each product field.

Characteristics of the less familiar markets beyond Europe are summarised briefly. As an example, in the final chapter of the book Equipped 4 reports on its experiences of exploiting technology in China.

A WORD FROM THE PUBLISHER

In bringing together leading organisations, ICC, CISP and BExA and practitioners to address the 2020 frontline issue of driving forward the UK's export performance, the University of Buckingham Press offers its thanks to all contributors. Their contact details are provided at the end of the book, and readers who want to learn more are invited to be in touch.

Jonathan Reuvid
Editor

LIST OF CONTRIBUTORS

Duncan Brock is a member of the leadership team of CIPS. His main role as Group Director is to ensure that CIPS provides its corporate and public sector customers globally with products and services that help them develop and improve their procurement and supply team's capabilities. In addition, he is responsible for increasing the number of offices and partners that CIPS has globally, with a particular focus this year on the USA. Duncan has over 30 years' procurement experience as a change driver, working with senior executives and procurement leadership teams in the design and modification of business-wide procurement processes and delivering improved business benefits. He's had a specific interest throughout his career on implementing category management and developing the skills and capabilities of procurement teams. His procurement experience comes from working for Ford, Mars, Black & Decker, NTL (now Virgin Media) and RSA. As a senior consultant he worked for QP and Future Purchasing with clients such as Diageo, Barclays & Nestlé. Duncan regularly chairs and presents at procurement and supply conferences and forums and is a spokesperson for CIPS for media interviews.

Marcus Dolman is Vice President, ECA Sales & Sales Finance, Rolls-Royce plc. He was appointed Co-Chairman of the British Exporters Association (BExA) in 2016 with specific responsibility for the Large Exporter members. He has been the Rolls-Royce representative at BExA since 2013 and was previously Chairman of the Industry Committee. Marcus is the focal point for all of Rolls-Royce Group's ECA activity, including maintaining the relationship with various government ECA departments, specifically UKEF, US EXIM and GIEK in Norway. He is also responsible for all Customer Financing activity in the Americas and Europe for Rolls-Royce's aerospace customers and globally for any land-based power projects. He obtained an MBA form the Open University in 2004 as part of the Rolls-Royce Management Development Curriculum.

Dr Barbara Ghinelli is the Director of Harwell Campus Cluster Development at Harwell Science and Innovation Campus, Oxfordshire, the UK's centre for scientific research and applied technology. She has established a high profile for the Space and the Health Rec Clusters and is leading the development of new Clusters, including Energy Tec. Barbara joined STFC in 2010 as Executive Director of Business Development. Successes included the creation of ISIC (now Satellite Application Catapult) at Harwell and of the High Performance Computing Centre (Hartree) at Daresbury. Previously, she worked at EA (now Airbus DS), where she managed business development across Europe for the €3.2 billion joint ESA/EU Earth Observation Programme for Global Monitoring of Environment and Security (now Copernicus) and secured a number of large contracts. She graduated in Electronic Engineering at the University of York, completed her PhD in Artificial Intelligence and Radar Imaging at the University of Sheffield and holds a Certificate in Management from the Open University.

Dr Mark Graves gained a first-class MEng degree in Electronic and Structural Materials Engineering from Oxford University, where he won the Maurice Lubbock prize in the final year examinations, and a PhD in Computer Science from the University of Wales, Cardiff, winning a Royal Commission 1851 Industrial Fellowship. Mark spent 20 years running engineering and software development projects with teams in Europe, the USA and India in fields ranging from food manufacturing control to wireless sensor networks. He is the named inventor of 4 granted patents, has published 10 academic papers and book chapters in the field of machine vision and is co-editor of the book *Machine Vision for Inspection of Natural Products*. Mark moved into the R&D Tax Credit and Patent Advisory field in 2010 and has since prepared over 700 technical claim reports in technologies ranging from software/IT, electronics and mechanical engineering through to food production and beauty products. He is a part-qualified patent attorney, having completed a post-graduate certificate in Intellectual Property Law from Bournemouth University and qualified as a Certified Patent Valuation Analyst, and has advised on and written patents for many companies including leading x-ray engineering and medical device patents. Mark is an active investor himself in early-stage technology companies, having shareholdings in more than 25.

Margit Hoehne is CEO of patentGate GmbH since 2008. She has 20 years' experience with patent information, starting as a research assistant at PATON, the patent information centre in Ilmenau, Germany.

Since then she has specialised in developing solutions for in-house patent monitoring workflows. Margit has a degree in business and computer science from the Technical University Ilmenau.

Natalia Korek is an IP strategist and Director for Basck, an Intellectual Property Consultancy specialising in building commercially focused IP portfolios for fast-growing brands and tech companies. Her focus is on assisting clients to develop and manage their IP assets from the brand perspective to maintain competitive advantage, especially for anti-counterfeiting purposes. Natalia holds a Master of Laws degree from the University of Wrocław and has previous experience of working with Big 4 consultancies, as well as in start-ups herself.

Julia May is a prize-winning Chartered Accountant and Chartered Tax Advisor, formerly an Arthur Andersen corporation tax specialist. She has a BEng Honours Degree in Engineering Science from the University of Liverpool, specialising in electrical, nuclear and mechanical engineering, and broad-based industry experience working for a number of software and IT consultancy firms before moving into the R&D Tax Credit field. One of the UK's leading R&D Tax Credit tax advisors, a delegate of the HMRC's Research & Development Consultative Committee and a member of the HMTC i-File Working Party, Julia has personally prepared and reviewed hundreds of R&D tax credit and, more recently, Patent Box claims. Specialising in handling HMRC inquiries on issues ranging from complications over offshore shareholder structures and taxation of capitalisation of intangible assets to basics such as inadequate record-keeping, Julia offers financial, tax modelling, fundraising and EIS or SEIS investment advice to a number of early-stage technology companies, where she is able to provide clients and their accountants with pragmatic commercial advice when faced with multiple interactive issues, always prioritising the overall needs of the business holistically.

Dr Brian More works as Director for Intellectual Property Commercialisation at Coventry University with responsibility for policy, protection, valuation and commercialisation of all forms of IP. He manages a portfolio of 20 patent families, 31 trademarks, designs and copyright. He has had 45 years' experience working with Intellectual Property, as inventor on 6 patents and jointly owned 4 trademarks. Brian has been active in starting 28 companies, using IP and attracting investment in them. Brian studied for a PhD in Grenoble as an employee of the CEA and subsequently worked at the NPL and BNFL's Company Research Laboratory. Prior to joining Coventry

University, he worked as Business Development Manager for the School of Physics and Astronomy at the University of Birmingham. He is a director of 4 companies and sits on 3 national advisory panels. Brian has worked for private contractors on assessment of development proposals in the field of nanotechnology and on EU Framework projects as commercialisation consultant. He has an MBA in Technology Transfer and Innovation from Coventry University and was awarded the 2009 Lord Stafford Award for Technology Transfer. He is currently an Innovate UK scale-up director specialising in IP strategy and valuation.

Simon Reeves specialises in Intellectual Property. After obtaining a Law Degree from Birmingham University in the UK, Simon joined Withers & Rogers, Patent and Trademark Agents in 1987 and in 1989 moved into the commercial sector with Unilever PLC as a Trademarks Manager. He then joined the alcoholic beverage company Allied Domecq PLC, where he became Head of the Group Trademarks Department in 1995. In 2004 Simon moved to the pharmaceutical sector joining AstraZeneca as Director of Trademarks. In 2010 he relocated to Basel to head up the Trademark Department of Syngenta, the global seeds and agrochemical company. Simon is a qualified barrister and also a qualified member by examination of ITMA where he spent four years as a Council Member. He is a past President of ECTA (the European Community Trade Mark Association) and a member of the following Associations: MARQUES, INTA, TMPDF and AIM.

Jonathan Reuvid is an editor and author of business books and a partner in Legend Times Group. He has been writing and editing books on international trade and investment for more than 25 years and has more than 80 editions of over 30 titles to his name as editor and co-author, including *The Handbook of International Trade*, *The Handbook of World Trade*, *Managing Cybersecurity Risk* and business guides to China, the 10 countries that joined the EU in 2004, South Africa and Morocco. Before taking up a second career in business publishing, Jonathan was Director of European Operations of the manufacturing subsidiaries of a Fortune 500 multinational. From 1984 to 2005 he engaged in joint venture development and start-ups in China. He is also a founder director of IPR Events, the quality exhibition organiser and President of the charity, Community First Oxfordshire.

Susan Ross is an Account Director at Aon Credit International, where she is an export credit insurance broker. She places risk in the London market, wholesale market, whole turnover market and with UK Export

Finance (UKEF). Susan chaired BExA from 2009 to 2012, during which time she successfully campaigned for the re-launch of the UKEF Bond Support scheme. In addition she introduced and edited several of the well-regarded series of BExA Guides, which provide exporters with practical and concise instructions on various export related subjects. Susan continues to be an active member of BExA, and was awarded an MBE in the Queen's Birthday Honours 2017 for voluntary services to UK exports.

Dominic Schiller is a UK and European Patent and Trademark Attorney with over 30 years' experience. He has a Master's in Business Administration and works closely with corporate finance organisations, technology due diligence experts and business incubators and accelerators in the UK and China. He founded his own patent and trademark firm Equipped 4 (IP) Limited and is an investor, and the in-house adviser, to several IP-rich technology companies, operating across a diverse range of industries including manufacturing, healthcare, pharmaceuticals and the creative industries. He has managed international collaborations, licensing and joint ventures with both large and small entities.

Dominic also runs Partner Investment with Ning Qu, a leading medical doctor and Professor with services between China, Europe and Australia and is currently working on creating a China/Europe/Australia investment fund to support their exiting cross-country activities.

Chris Southworth is Secretary General at the International Chamber of Commerce UK and a regular voice for business in the international media. He is founder of the ICC Digital Trade Roadmap and a member of the ICC G7, G20, Digitisation and Ecommerce Working Groups and ICC World Council, as well as the International Advisory Boards of the Digital Trade Network and Queen Mary-UNIDROIT Institute of Transnational Commercial Law. Prior to joining ICC, he was Executive Director for Global Partnerships, at the British Chambers of Commerce, Head of the International Chambers of Commerce Unit at UK Trade and Investment (UKTI) and a Senior Policy Advisor to Lord Heseltine for his independent review of UK competitiveness. In 2011 he helped set up the mid-size business export programme at UKTI and was a Senior Policy Advisor for the 2011 Government Review of Mid-Size Businesses. Former roles have encompassed deregulatory and social enterprise policy at the Department for Business and stints improving public services at local strategic partnership level and the NGO sector.

Olaf Swanzy is the PNO Group UK sector specialist for innovation with close working relationships with all principal funding bodies in this sector. He joined the PNO Group in 2004 to help establish the UK operation with an initial focus on technology development within the Environmental Sector. Over the past 15 years, Olaf has worked with an extensive range of SMEs and large companies across all industry sectors and academia to advance research and innovation activities through the procurement of government funding from national and EU sources. Since 2008, he has been involved in the delivery of training for SMEs in the area of government funding for innovative investment activities. Olaf has retired recently as Managing Director but continues to act as a consultant to PNO.

Terry Toms is Founder and Managing Director of RandDTax, which provides consultancy services to assess and scope research and development for tax credit claims, working mainly with innovative SMEs, accountancy practices and trade bodies. Terry has a background in the IT software sector running a UK development and marketing team, then consulting with software businesses, having initially qualified in banking. He has been an active member of the HMRC Research and Development Consultative committee for the last seven years and has advised companies since 2002. Since he founded RandDTax in 2012, the company has helped over 1,200 companies gain in excess of £131 million in R&D tax credits, through in excess of 5,000 claims. RandDTax now has 30 Consultants across the UK (of whom 19 are shareholders), and 12 directors. The RandDTax team of experts offer an unrivalled service through a hands-on approach, specialist tax and technical knowledge and a strong relationship with HMRC. In 2017, RandDTax won the Business Innovation Award at the National SME Business Awards. This award-winning formula is used on a daily basis to help businesses across a very broad range of industry sectors.

Glynis Whiting is Managing Partner at TIAO and a founding partner in two startups providing digital transformation for membership organisations and companies. She has 30 years' leadership experience in EU and UK public policy, business development, innovation and high impact projects to address global challenges. A resident of Brussels, Glynis set up West Midlands in Europe in 2000 with over 90 stakeholder partners. She is a founder member of the European Regions Research and Innovation Network and former President of the British Chamber of Commerce in Belgium.

PART ONE
ENCOURAGING INNOVATORS

1.1

SPACE, HEALTH AND ENERGY – HOW MULTI-SECTORAL COLLABORATION IS FUELLING INNOVATION

Dr Barbara Ghinelli, Harwell Science and Innovation Campus

It is not uncommon for technology originally developed in one sector to find application in other industries. As a sector blooms, so does the pressure to innovate, and this creates a rich source of technology that becomes more accessible to communities outside of specialist teams. Opportunities for putting the technology to use in other industries accelerates considerably, resulting in the creation of new businesses and opening up new market opportunities for companies in those sectors.

An oft-quoted example is the Apollo moon programme, and today the space sector is again experiencing rapid growth in relation to investment and commercial interest as the possibilities and opportunities it wields become more widely known. Increasingly it is realised that science and technology should not be siloed, and healthcare and energy are two sectors taking full advantage of the opportunities for collaboration that this approach presents. Examples include the European Space Agency (ESA) developing suits with embedded biomedical sensors to study how the human body responds to living in space – technology that led to the creation of a baby monitoring system to protect against cot deaths. Similarly, microbiological sensors for space applications are being used to detect contamination for better water treatment, and NASA's handling of hydrogen paved the way for developing light-weight hydrogen tanks for environmentally friendly cars.

Innovative thinkers and business leaders are no strangers to seeing the potential of technology from one sector being applied to another. Looking further into the crossover between space and health technology, there are applications in ultra-light robots for surgery and the production of artificial organs and prostheses. Previous uses also include a 'pill camera' developed by researchers at the Fraunhofer Institute that can be swallowed by patients, dementia-tracking slippers which use GPS, and technology developed for space travel being used for breast-screening vans.

Technologies developed for the space sector are improving our daily lives and, as they rapidly pervade the healthcare sector and others, we are beginning to see more cases that demonstrate its positive presence, and positive return for the businesses with the vision to seize on these commercial opportunities. For example, earlier this year the UK Space Agency granted Adaptix £1m in funding to develop a pioneering portable 3D medical X-ray machine, based on technology used to study stars in distant galaxies. Working on Harwell Science and Innovation Campus, the scientists realised that, as well as providing access to previously unreachable parts of our universe, the technology will allow doctors to get a more comprehensive view of areas where they suspect tumours are growing, aiding more effective treatment and earlier diagnosis. Health and space-heritage technology may seem an unlikely partnership, but it is one that has led directly to life-saving technology and commercial returns.

Many other examples exist where technology originally developed for space exploration has been put to good use in healthcare. For instance, by adapting a small 3D Camera originally designed for investigating scientific samples on the moon, start-up 3D-oscopy has created an endoscope camera that can quickly record and digitally recreate a human digestive tract. For the clinicians, it means they can examine detailed footage of the tract off-line, rather than in real-time while the camera is inside the patient, with quantification tools to further inform their recommendations on surgery and treatments. For the patients, this means endoscopy time is drastically reduced, only requiring the camera to make one pass into and out of the tract, recording all and any features. For the health-care system, it means shorter waiting times, more efficient use of funds and better patient outcomes.

It is not only *hardware* that businesses should be looking at when it comes to innovating, but also the use of satellite-derived data, originally gathered with one use in mind but which can be repurposed. siHealth are one example of a company successfully combining satellite and ground-based data to improve health outcomes. They use satellite observations of Earth to allow people to manage their exposure to sunlight through a smartphone app. Exposure to sunlight brings risks and benefits – too little or too much can be bad for your health. Each person's skin requires and tolerates different

amounts of sunlight based on demographics such as age, skin-tone and lifestyle. Localised pollution can also work with the sunlight to increase damage, resulting in a complex series of factors which make it difficult for individuals to manage their exposure unaided. siHealth has recently announced a strategic alliance with BASF to use their app as part of a system to monitor the absorption and effectiveness of various medical skin creams.

In another example, the UK's National Health Service has a shortage of doctors to staff local medical practices, leading to significant issues for some regions. This can lead to ailments becoming more severe than they would if treated quickly, and can add strain to local hospitals when patients access the healthcare system via Accident and Emergency units, unable to book appointments at their local doctor's surgery. TekiHealth, a company established by two doctors, has devised a remote diagnostic solution. Through satellite technology it has provided high-bandwidth links that allows people to be examined at their local doctor's surgery by a qualified medical doctor located elsewhere. This modern approach to the doctor-patient consultation is alleviating delays caused by shortage of local staff and improving patient outcomes.

CREATING NEW MARKET OPPORTUNITIES

Cross-sector collaboration creates opportunities in new markets. Though not developed for space applications, Oxford Nanopore's portable gene sequencer, MinION, is an example of the kind of technology that will be needed to support future space habitats. MinION has been used on the International Space Station to sequence both DNA and RNA. This can, for example, be used to identify microorganisms that might develop onboard so as to be able to mitigate any harmful effects they might cause, as well as to monitor changes in human health or microbiomes in response to spaceflight, and to conduct biomedical research in microgravity. Devices such as this will become ever more important in maintaining isolated, closed environments, be they in a spacecraft or on an extra-terrestrial body. As such ventures become more common and extensive, they are very likely to become technology drivers that will result in unexpected benefits here on Earth.

The value of cross-collaboration of space technology in other industries beyond just healthcare has also become very apparent. For example, the energy sector is adopting space technology to build better clean energy systems and solutions that have a positive environmental impact.

Mirico, an SME based within Harwell Campus, is one example of a company that has successfully taken technology developed for space and applied it to the energy sector. In developing its laser gas-sensing technology, originally designed to measure atmospheric constituents in space, it found that the technology could be perfectly deployed to accurately measure atmospheric pollutants for energy companies, helping them to determine where to focus their efforts in improving the efficiency and safety of operations.

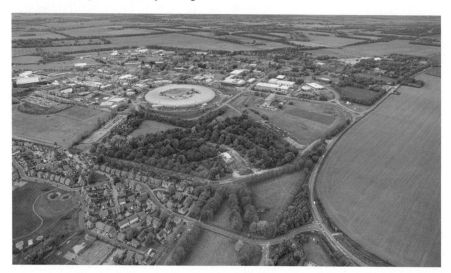

It is evident, therefore, that taking an innovative, cross-industry approach to problem solving in energy and environmental issues is effective, as in the case of Mirico, which repurposed a technology developed as a result of more than ten years of cutting-edge Earth observation and planetary exploration.

EMBRACING TRANSFORMATION

The worlds of science and technology already intersect with every industry, sector and aspect of life. In the case of healthcare, a report by Aruba predicts the next five to ten years will see massive disruptions in this arena, with artificial intelligence playing an increasing role in diagnosis and treatment by 2030.

Technologies or applications being used in this sector are testament to the powerful advantage of working in close proximity with organisations outside a sector's usual market – through shared learning and collaboration, new business opportunities are identified and innovative solutions to long standing problems are created. This is a huge advantage more generally and one that will continue to grow and develop.

To truly thrive, it is important for collaboration to be diverse, and that the public sector is closely linked with fast-growth SMEs and multinationals. This way, we can better collaborate, co-fund and problem-solve; ultimately developing innovative technologies that create new markets, resulting in job creation and economic growth.

1.2

BUSINESS GROWTH THROUGH INDUSTRY-ACADEMIA INTERACTIONS

Dr Brian More, Coventry University

INTRODUCTION

In 2016 on writing the first version of this chapter I alluded to global challenges as we entered the Brexit and Trump eras. The reality of the ensuing years has astonished most seasoned PESTEL analysts as Political, Economic, Social, Technological, Environmental and Legal paradigms changed rapidly, and indicate clearly that industry-academic collaborations and partnerships are a preferred, if not essential, way to solve these complex interrelated global issues.

Technological advances in 5G, mobile internet, cloud technology, processing power of big data, internet of things (IoT), artificial intelligence, augmented reality, robotics and machine learning in the fourth industrial revolution (4IR) has led to the World Economic Forum[1] classifying the following 10 skills/competences necessary for any organisation and individual for prosperity in the next decade.

Each one of these competences is greatly enhanced by using the 10 industry-academia interactions which follow; some new interactions have been added and others enhanced by specific examples of best practice.

1. Complex Problem-Solving
2. Critical Thinking
3. Creativity
4. People Management
5. Coordinating with Others
6. Emotional Intelligence
7. Judgement and Decision-Making
8. Service Orientation
9. Negotiation
10. Cognitive Flexibility

In the United Kingdom universities are seen as essential pillars in the communities in which they reside, offering services not witnessed before as they strive to provide a central focus for society. In 2018 the Knowledge Exchange Framework (KEF)[2] was piloted in England with the aim of increasing efficiency and effectiveness in use of public funding for knowledge exchange (KE), to further a culture of continuous improvement in universities by providing a package of support to keep English university knowledge exchange operating at a world class standard. It aims to address the full range of KE activities displayed on a radar chart, where university performances can be compared.

Industry will then have data to show where each English university sits with respect to others in research (REF), teaching (TEF) and knowledge exchange (KEF), enabling them to select the right one for any intended outcome.

Many universities are classified as large businesses with turnover exceeding £500 million, and provide far more services than just teaching and research to businesses, charities and Government organisations. Universities are seen not only as a source of young talent for business but a cost-effective way of industry improving both products and services, discovering new technologies and building upon the skill base of employees. Government sees the universities as prime locations for funding to develop new products and deliver business services to industry. From a theoretical collaborative business model to delivery of tangible results the Triple Helix[3] of Government/Academia/Industry interaction is starting to deliver impact for many countries.

Academic-Industry interactions are naturally two-way, companies of all sizes and legal structures can support the Governments research and education agenda by providing more industry and societal challenges to drive relevant and focused research. As the skills needs of new business sectors change, the academic base has to be responsive to provide these skills at the right level and right time for global growth in international markets.

Industry has to compete in the global marketplace as international political changes since 2016 have simultaneously opened up opportunities, and closed doors, to trade and commerce. As UK Government focus shifts towards scale-up business support to grow our economy, no matter what the size of the industry or the state and stage of their development, a collaborative approach to working with academia is recommended.

Internationally developed economies approach industry-academia interactions in essentially the same way, with the trade-off between freedom of publication and intellectual property lock-up the most cited area of conflict.[4] Out of Canada, Japan, the UK and USA only Japan permits companies to control exclusively most collaborative inventions and to censor academic publications. Even in this situation companies are reported as not developing university discoveries to their full potential.

This is a practical chapter aimed to articulate current academia-industry interactions, and offer some guidance as to benefits and challenges going forward.

ACADEMIC-INDUSTRY INTERACTIONS MAKE A DIFFERENCE

One of the latest and most influential reports on the evidence underpinning industry-academic research collaborations is the 2015 Dowling Report[5] issued by the UK Government. Both qualitative and quantitative evidence demonstrate why it is important for both sectors to collaborate to improve their respective businesses. Ideas and creativity from both industry and academia, and more importantly the multidisciplinary collaboration between both, creates new products, processes, services and business models. Early pre-competitive research and an open innovation approach involving many companies and universities has proven to increase innovation through sharing of research results, for example the Structural Genomics Consortium.[6]

In the Dowling Report the UK Government recognises the importance of their role in providing strategic leadership and financial support to collaborations in order to drive economic growth. For every pound spent by Innovate UK on collaborative research the gross value added (GVA) was £9.67 where there were 2 or more academic partners, compared to £4.22 without academic partners. Businesses which invest more in R&D are on average 13% more productive than those with no R&D spend; these innovating businesses also see additional benefits in that they are more likely to:

- Be active exporters and achieve better value added per employee.

- Exhibit faster growth. It has been estimated that 51% of labour productivity growth between 2000 and 2008 could be attributed to innovation.
- As collaborators produce higher quality research outputs than research conducted either within an individual firm, or on an academic basis alone.

Conversely, for academic researchers the benefits reported included the following;

- Gaining real industry problems to solve, automatic relevance of research.
- Benefiting from working with other disciplines on industry projects.
- Increasing the breadth and reach of funding opportunities.
- Making a positive difference to society, providing their work with meaning and purpose to make a positive difference.
- Accessing new networks.
- Witnessing laboratory research go to industrial scale.
- Seeing new technologies reach the marketplace.
- Seeing societal impact from academic research, theory to practice.

WAYS OF INTERACTING WITH INDUSTRY

Two of the major barriers reported by industry in engaging with universities was the lack of a clear entry point to start the dialogue, and no clarity of the potential benefits. These issues have been overcome by most UK universities with dedicated business-facing support teams having an associated contact website. Figure 1.2.1. illustrates Coventry University's contact details shown on social media.

Figure 1.2.1 – Coventry University's Twitter Cover Image

Source: Coventry University, Enterprise & Innovation

Before industry collaborates with a university the following points, taken from the Dowling Report, are considered to be important in achieving success, for all parties concerned:

- Strong and trusting personal relationships;
- Shared vision, goals and objectives defined, setting in place clear expectations;
- Mutual understanding between partners;
- Ability of, and opportunities for, staff to work across institutional boundaries;
- Collaboration brings about mutual benefits;
- Available funding;
- Processes for agreeing contracts and IP are in place;
- Clear and effective communication between partners;
- Organisational support, including senior management buy-in and championing of projects;
- Willingness to devote time and resources from both parties.

These points for success are mirrored in the USA[7] with additional emphasis placed upon:

- Identification of leaders who are capable of crossing boundaries between business and academia to foster strong ties.
- Investment in long-term relationships. A long-term relationship allows parties to share risk and accountability without overburdening a single entity. Under a shared vision and a foundation of mutual trust, a long-term partnership can reap great results by building a body of work over time.

Most industry-academic engagements start with a single project whereby both parties gain trust. If this interaction meets both parties' expectations and outcomes then multiple projects lead to larger collaborative research, strategic partnerships and other large-scale projects. For strategic partnerships universities and industry partners will employ a dedicated client manager to deal with all interactions or touch points between partners.

For practical purposes interactions fall within 10 distinct but not mutually exclusive categories as below:

a) Collaborative projects and partnerships
In collaborative projects and partnerships, costs are usually shared between parties because each will benefit from the collaboration, e.g. developing a new product, process or service for the industrial

partner based upon applied research. Once the intellectual property has been protected by the industry or academic partner, then publications disseminate the results as widely as possible. Often the industry costs are subsidised by Government grants and/or academic partner contributions. In addition to publications, dependent upon the collaboration contract, the academic partner may receive an on-going royalty payment through a commercial licence for product sales. To support collaborative research some businesses, fund a chair at a university, or an honorary professor is located in academia.

In 2019 Coventry University's Institute for Advanced Manufacturing and Engineering (AME) was awarded a prestigious Queen's Anniversary Prize. AME is a unique partnership between Coventry University and Unipart Manufacturing Group; it is located on the leading international manufacturer's site in Coventry. Known as the 'Faculty on the Factory Floor', it allows students to engage directly with the engineering and manufacturing industry to the benefit of themselves and the industry as a whole.

AME develops skilled graduate engineers to address the growing skills shortage in the engineering and manufacturing sector.

In addition to this, there is a team of technology specialists and professors who are working together to develop new power-train and clean energy solutions for the transport sector. Projects have included light-weight exhaust systems, fuel tanks for hybrid vehicles and battery energy storage systems working with a number of leading automotive companies.

Benefits for business include:

- Future access to industry-ready engineering graduates;
- Benefit from cutting-edge research on new technologies;
- Enhanced knowledge transfer opportunities;
- Driving forward growth technologies in key global markets.

b) Contract research

In cases where the industrial partner needs to own and control the use of intellectual property from the academic partner then contract research is used. Industry generally will be expected to pay the full economic costs for the research, and their expectation is that the contract will be professionally managed and delivered to industry standards of time and quality.

c) Continuing Professional Development (CPD)

Continuing Professional Development (CPD) of staff is a key differentiator for industry in growing and competing in the commercial world. Universities deliver accredited CPD courses in most industrially relevant subjects from law, engineering, sciences, leadership, languages and management. Courses are delivered in all the required media formats and locations to meet industry needs – at the university, at the industrial site, at residential locations and more frequently online. CPD courses and seminars are also delivered by industry, providing an opportunity for academic staff to maintain and build on their knowledge and skills. CPD courses are an excellent way of staff networking and for building lasting relationships on both sides. In addition to CPD, industry/academic staff secondments are a very popular way to build partnerships and expose staff to respective working environments, processes, procedures and priorities. CPD is now much easier with online courses, the benefits of which are:

Flexibility   By having access to the internet, students' study whenever and wherever they want.

Value   Cost can be spread by a flexible pay-per-module payment option.

Community   Truly international in scope, learning with over 8 million across the world and growing.

Coventry University, ranked 4th in the first ever global university rankings for online courses,[8] currently offer 15 degree programmes and 75 courses on the FutureLearn platform, covering MBA, MSc, PSE, undergraduate and PGCert courses.[9]

d) Expert consultancy, practical problem-solving

Expert consultancy is where industry wants to access the expertise of certain academics when they have an urgent problem which needs solving, in the short term rather than through long or medium term research. The consultancy contracts would be expected to be paid for in full by the industry requesting the service. Examples here might be engineering expertise when a process line fails, or for expert witnesses in court cases. Academic consultants are also used widely for business advice and in the medical sector. This is a feature of industry working with academia for complex problem solving, the number one World Economic Forum necessary skill.

e) Business space and conferencing facilities

Larger universities run incubator, accelerator and co-working spaces for business to locate, work and access academic expertise. These science or technology parks provide both laboratory and office space for spin-out and spin-in companies, often accompanied by large conference centres and meeting rooms. Science and technology parks are also run by industry and will have a specific sector focus, often dictated by the anchor industry, for example pharmaceutical companies (Cambridge BioPharma Cluster[10]), environmental (Hong Kong Science Park[11]) or digital industry (Stanford Research Park, California[12]). Clustering businesses in a sector on a science park, located at or near a university or universities, is a well-documented method of creating value in cities and regions. Running a shared science park with academia and industry co-located creates a hotbed of ideas from cross-disciplinary contacts. Science and Technology parks will benefit from having venture capital co-location to fund innovations and growing businesses; Stanford for example has the wealth of Silicon Valley to access.

f) Access to funding

Hundreds of funding schemes are available for industrial-academic collaborations, particularly in the field of pre-competitive research, for example national (Innovate UK), regional (Northern Powerhouse, Midland Engine), sub-regional (Local Enterprise Partnerships), European (Horizon 2020, Europe Enterprise Network) and international (Research Councils UK, the Newton Fund, the Industry Engagement Fund). Businesses who collaborate with universities can often use university specialist teams of bid writers who can support them gain access to grants, debt and equity finance. The industry-academic landscape for interactions remains complex (as seen in figure 1.2.2 below), so care needs to be taken in using the right scheme for specific desired outcomes.

Figure 1.2.2 – Research and Innovation landscape Map (Taken from the Dowling Report[2])

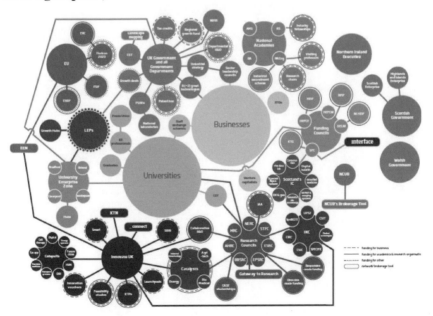

Source: The Dowling Review of Business-University Business Research Collaborations, 2015, www.raeng.org.uk/publications/reports/ the-dowling-review-of-business-university-research

The Department for Business, Energy and Industrial Strategy (BEIS) simplified this somewhat in April 2018 by combining the seven research councils responsible for university research funding with Research England and Innovate UK, responsible for innovation across industry and academia. The new UKRI (UK Research and Innovation) structure is seen in figure 1.2.3. The aim here is to provide a seamless service from funding of research through to the scaling-up of businesses across all sectors, by maximising the contribution of each of the component parts, working individually and collectively.

The UK Government has put research and innovation at the heart of its Industrial Strategy, setting an ambition for the UK to become the most innovative country in the world and increase its total R&D expenditure to 2.4% of GDP by 2027 partnered by UKRI.

Figure 1.2.3 – The Structure of UK Research and Innovation (UKRI), working to increase R&D expenditure to 2.4% of GDP by 2027

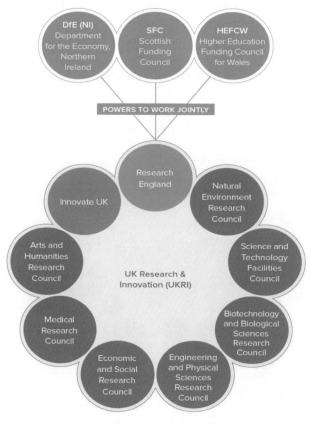

Source: Academy of Medical Sciences, British Academy, Royal Academy of Engineering and Royal Society, 2018

g) Access to intellectual property

Intellectual property opens up the opportunities for both parties for economic growth. However, IP ownership, use and commercial terms need to be well thought out for both industry and academia when collaborating on projects. This is still the most significant barrier to industry collaborating with academia, and the second most significant barrier for academia collaborating with industry. To help in reaching mutually acceptable terms for IP the Lambert Agreements[13] have been drafted by legal experts in consultation with industry and academia. These agreements have recently been updated and are a good starting point for negotiations, but will require amendments, additions and deletions for each specific contract. Most industry-academic interactions are not single negotiations, but rather an expectation of a longer-term relationship. With this in mind, both parties need flexibility in ensuring a win-win scenario is in place, and professional negotiating courses will facilitate this process.

h) Access to talent, student placements, internships and recruitment

Talent remains the foundation upon which national industrial growth depends. Many universities have regional schemes to enable easy access to students and staff as part of their commitment to the community. Industry has an important role to play in specifying the sector-specific skills and expertise they require. By listening to industry the UK Government and academic institutions have responded to industry need and has led to degree apprenticeships, and more tailored industry specific courses, as below:

Coventry University deliver Higher and Degree Apprenticeships in partnership with industry; the degree apprenticeships are now popular among students who do not want to stack up debt whilst at university. The programmes are tailored to enable access at various levels and can be completed in either 48 months, 32 months or 16 months dependent on entry point.

i) Knowledge Transfer Partnerships (KTPs')[14]

Knowledge Transfer Partnerships is a UK-wide programme that has been helping businesses for the past 40 years to improve their competitiveness and productivity through the better use of knowledge, technology and skills that reside within the UK Knowledge Base (usually a university).

A Knowledge Transfer Partnership serves to meet a core strategic need and to identify innovative solutions to help that business grow. KTP often delivers significant increased profitability for business partners as a direct result of the partnership through improved quality and operations, increased sales and access to new markets. A KTP Associate is employed by a university partner, but the associate works full time at the industry partner to transfer their knowledge to the company. A KTP is subsidised by the UK Government and has widely been used by commercial and non-commercial organisations.

In 2019 BEIS introduced a KTP for management, aimed at increasing SME company level productivity; this followed global productivity gap analysis. The programme runs from 2019 to 2022 with £25 million of funding to deliver 200 management focused KTP projects. In addition to increasing the company's productivity through strategic management change the project will provide added value to academia through research data. These will be delivered in business with academic supervision through business schools and management faculties.

Source: Knowledge Transfer Partnerships, ktp.innovateuk.org/

j) Access to state-of-the-art equipment

State-of-the-art equipment is made available both in industry and academic institutions. Catapult Centres[15] are a recent attempt to drive good research results through technology transfer to market; they have been set up to support industry in the eight great technologies identified as important to the growth of the UK economy. Similar centres found in Germany are the Fraunhofer-Gesellschaft[16] institutes.

CONCLUSIONS

Many examples and case studies exist to demonstrate the importance, significance and impact of industry-academic collaborations and partnerships. This includes for example the REF Impact Case Studies,[17] a collection of 6,975 case studies submitted by UK universities under the research excellence framework in 2014, and the University Industry Innovation Network good practice series 2016.[18]

Good partnerships and collaborations can be long-lasting and rewarding; many are characterised by committed individuals and champions on both sides. Challenges tend to arise where the driving force behind the collaboration moves on, where university researchers fail to appreciate the commercial drivers for industrial work or where an industry strategy changes rapidly. Strategic differences for each sector remain; however, the interaction between both is improving as the academic sector employ teams who cross the boundary to specifically grow partnerships.

Today, more than ever, it's time industry started to work closer with the academic base, and universities listen harder to the real world needs of industry to ensure a prosperous and sustainable future.

The opportunities for industry-academia collaboration and partnership are numerous and varied, they include working towards achieving the millennium goal targets and supporting the delivery of global 'Lighthouse Projects'.

REFERENCES

1. The World Economic Forum, 'The Future of Jobs', reports. weforum.org/future-of-jobs-2016/shareable-infographics
2. UKRI, Knowledge Exchange Framework, re.ukri.org/knowledge-exchange/knowledge-exchange-framework/
3. Infographics, triplehelix.stanford.edu/3helix_concept
4. 'Industry-University Collaborations in Canada, Japan, the UK and USA – with Emphasis on Publication Freedom and Managing the Intellectual Property Lock-up Problem', journals.plos.org/plosone/article?id=10.1371/journal.pone.0090302
5. The Dowling Review of Business-University Business Collaborations, 2015, www.bis.gov.uk
6. The Structural Genomics Consortium, www.thesgc.org/
7. 'How Academic Institutions Partner with Private Industry', www.rdmag.com/article/2015/04/how-academic-institutions-partner-private-industry
8. 'First Ever World University Rankings Based On MOOC Performance Unveiled', www.prnewswire.com/news-releases/first-ever-world-university-rankings-based-on-mooc-performance-unveiled-300963685.html
9. Coventry University Online Learning, www.coventry.ac.uk/study-at-coventry/online-learning/
10. Bidwells Cambridge BioPharma Cluster, www.bidwells.co.uk/assets/Uploads/downloads/biopharma-clusters/research-biopharma-cluster-cambridge-report-rebrand.pdf

11. Hong Kong Science and Technology Park, www.hkstp.org/hkstp_web/en/what-we-do/innovation-for-a-brighter-future/clusters-in-focus/Green%20Technology
12. Stanford Research Park, www.stanfordresearchpark.com/
13. University and Business Collaboration Agreements: The Lambert Toolkit, www.gov.uk/guidance/university-and-business-collaboration-agreements-lambert-toolkit
14. Knowledge Transfer Partnerships, ktp.innovateuk.org/
15. Catapult Centres, catapult.org.uk/
16. Fraunhofer Institutes and Research Establishments, www.fraunhofer.de/en/institutes.html
17. REF Impact Case Studies, 2014, www.hefce.ac.uk/rsrch/refimpact/
18. *University Industry Innovation Network, Good Practice Guide 2016 Series: Fostering University-Industry relationships, Entrepreneurial Universities and Collaborative Innovation.* ISBN 978-94-91901-19-5

1.3

BRAND STRATEGY FOR SCALE-UPS – PROTECT YOUR VOICE

Simon Reeves and Natalia Korek, Basck

INTRODUCTION

Your brand is the voice of your company; it will reflect your goodwill and reputation built up as a result of years of hard work. What if you picked a voice at the outset that can be easily silenced or one that is heard differently depending on who is listening to it? Or a voice that can simply be lost in the crowd?

It is surprising to discover how many companies draw inspiration, either expressly or subliminally, from existing brands already recognised and advertised in their business area or a closely related business area when selecting a new brand name. Needless to say, those imitation brand names, if adopted, are likely to be silenced at birth by swift and successful legal action which will leave you out of pocket and right back where you started. Then there are those brands which sound fine in English, but speak with a very different voice when heard in another language. That said, surprisingly some prominent brands survive despite this oversight:

*Vauxhall/Opel **Nova**® for cars – where 'No va' in Spanish means 'does not go'*

Irish Mist® *for liqueurs – where 'Mist' in German means 'manure'*

Finally, there are brands whose voice can be lost in the crowd. Brands which are prone to falling into this category are those which are developed for products for short-term or seasonal lifecycles. This is seen frequently in industries such as cosmetics or fashion, where the tendency is to pick a name which is more descriptive of the look and feel of the product or the benefits it provides. A number of competing products jostle for position on the shelves, where the brands are made up of the same or very similar descriptive words and, as a result, their voices are diluted or weakened. They cease to be the voice which can clearly denote the origin of a particular product which is the essential function of a brand and its legal reflection, the trademark.

CREATION: THE VOICE THAT REFLECTS WHO YOU ARE, NOT WHAT YOU PROVIDE

When there are so many competing demands on the funds of an expanding business, it might be counter-intuitive to choose to set aside funds for a creative agency to help you create your brand(s) with you. However, developing the brand personality and the values you want your brand to represent from the outset will pay dividends in the medium to long term, generating the distinctive recognition, customer loyalty and goodwill behind the brand which will sustain your business development in both good as well as challenging economic circumstances.

For many FMCG brands, new brand creation will invariably result in highlighting some quality or benefit of your product or services in the name itself; the trick will be to ensure that the resulting name, even if containing a descriptive element, falls on the right side of the line, so that the selected name is also sufficiently legally strong to be enforceable against imitators and copycats. For this reason, it is important to ensure that you have a trademark advisor participating at the workshops with the branding agency to act as a foil to the creative professionals.

In more highly regulated industries, such as the pharmaceutical or agricultural industries, the ability to be creative around the choice of brand name is much more prescribed, because of the overriding imperative around patient/consumer safety; i.e. you cannot describe the efficacy or other characteristics of a product in the brand name if it has any potential to mislead. Hence the choice of brand names in these industries inevitably gravitates towards invented names, which are also made for the strongest legally enforceable trademarks.

CLEARANCE: THE VOICE THAT CAN BE HEARD

IP practitioners take various approaches to conducting trademark checks in the Trademark Registries in order to advise their clients as to their brand's availability for use and registration. Much is dictated by the budget a company has to invest behind those activities. The cost of full availability searches for a mark in multiple countries is likely to be more expensive than the cost of applying for and straightforward prosecution of the trademark through to registration in those same countries.

For a company with plans to expand in one or more markets outside its first core market, one approach is to carry out full searches in line with the timings of your launch plans in those countries with less rigorous searches (identical/near identical) in countries which are further down that launch plan. If all searches look fairly positive, then file trademark applications immediately in all countries searched. The advantage of this approach is that the registration process in the countries in which you have carried out the less rigorous searches will throw up any significant third-party trademarks as part of that process. In many countries you can obtain a registration within a year and you will know of any significant obstacles well before that.

This approach also works in regulated industries where the name has also to be approved as part of the regulatory process and the commercial launch of the product may be 5 or more years down the track from the time you are creating and clearing brand names. In those circumstances you will be searching for a first-choice brand name and several backup names and can allow for an attrition rate, either as a result of the regulatory or trademark registration process. The only difference in approach here is that you would carry out your full searches only in your must-have countries, which will probably, but may not necessarily, coincide with your list of first-to-launch countries.

The crucial point to note in this context is that the most important advice which is based on clearance searches is freedom to operate. If you launch your new brand in a country and are successfully sued in the courts of that country for trademark infringement, then a company will have to immediately cease use of that brand, withdraw all marketing and publicity already in circulation associated with that brand and pay damages to the successful party to compensate them for their loss of profits. It is therefore vital to create a branding strategy that does not only rely on the main brand name. Put the same emphasis on building and protecting your logos, straplines, product names, etc. Any of these might eventually become your fallback plan and allow your business smooth transition from one name to another, without losing a significant amount of goodwill accumulated in the previous name.

EXPANSION: THE VOICE THAT IS READY TO ECHO WITHOUT BORDERS

The trademark registries around the world are crowded, particularly when you are trying to protect trademarks in popular business sectors. For a scale-up company, the holy grail is to build and then protect a global brand, whatever that means for your business. At a minimum this will mean trading with a single brand in all the countries in which your products and services are on the market. The obvious reason for this is enhanced brand recognition which, in turn, increases bottom-line sales. It is rare that a company will achieve this holy grail without overcoming some legal challenges. Even the largest companies have not overcome insurmountable obstacles for some of their brands.

*The car brand is **VAUXHALL®** in some countries, **OPEL®** in others.*

***MARATHON®** chocolate bars are **SNICKERS®** chocolate bars in some countries.*

Some legal challenges are insurmountable; others can potentially be overcome during the prosecution process when they are raised as obstacles to registration. A good trademark attorney will use a variety of skills and tools in their toolkit to obtain commercially acceptable coexistence agreements with a third party which may be country or regionally specific or global in application.

REGISTRATION: THE VOICE THAT IS THE ONLY ONE LISTENED TO

A trademark registration gives the registered proprietor, on paper, the exclusive right to use the trademark for the goods and/or services for which it is registered. By definition, this is a monopoly right, which is the only form of intellectual property which can last forever, so long as the registration is renewed, usually at 10-year intervals. A portfolio of registered trademark registrations supported by commercialisation of the brand in the relevant countries can be a company's most valuable asset. In order to illustrate this, consider a theoretical investment decision which gave the investor the choice between purchasing the COCA-COLA® trademark portfolio together with the trade secret recipe for the soft drink as opposed to purchasing all the manufacturing sites and bottling plants which COCA-COLA® owns to produce and distribute the product. The right to affix the trademark COCA-COLA® to the drink as opposed to access to the means of manufacturing and distributing a generic product from those premises is likely to be far more valuable, even if the investor had to invest in new manufacturing facilities or license others to manufacture.

The challenge is to ensure that the company's trademark protection continues to reflect its commercial footprint as the company grows. To give sufficient attention to this, among all the other priorities, is a challenge by itself. New trademark applications must be placed on file well in advance of entering new markets. The more successful a brand becomes, the more likely an opportunist is to file a speculative trademark application for your brand and then attempt to hold you to ransom, demanding payment for its assignment back to your company.

In addition to securing all relevant trademarks, a company must not forget domain names. Register your top-level domain names (TLDs) and country-level domain names (CLDs) incorporating your brand names. The practice of domain-name squatting and extorting payment for the return of those domain names to their rightful owners, is rife. As opposed to what some entrepreneurs are led to believe: holding all domain names does not mean you do not need a trademark anymore. Similarly, having registration at Companies House is not considered an alternative to trademark rights, which are the only rights providing you with exclusivity to the name in the selected business fields.

MANAGEMENT: THE VOICE THAT DOES NOT NEED BACKUP SINGERS

The routine management of your registered rights means you will need to keep good records of the use of your brands. A certain percentage of your portfolio will fall due for renewal every year. This is not in all cases as simple as paying a fee; in some countries proof of use is required as a condition of renewal and, in others, additional supporting documentation. Every company should pay great attention to maintenance as, once rights are lost, it is not straightforward to restore them and third parties may well have already taken advantage of lapsed rights to jump in and file a trademark application for the brand for which you have done all the hard work to create and build a reputation.

As you build and develop the profile of your brand, it will pay dividends if you keep an eye on the competitor landscape. As a minimum you should be watching the publication of conflicting trademarks on the main national and multinational (e.g. European trademarks) registers so that you can challenge conflicting trademarks within the relevant prescribed timescales. You will probably need a similar watch service in place to alert you for conflicting domain names.

Counterfeiters will only reproduce branded products where they can make the highest profit margins on sales. Imitation is the sincerest form of flattery in this context and your brand has definitely met the threshold to merit this criminal activity if it is targeted by counterfeiters – this is not of much comfort of course! There are management tools you may wish to invest in which will trawl the internet and alert you to the sale of potential counterfeit/lookalike products. Online marketplaces have dedicated teams to deal with counterfeit claims but they will not take action unless your brand is registered as a trademark in the relevant country of issue. Likewise, if the look of your packaging is unique, register it as a design to allow for smooth handling of any counterfeit issue.

The principle advice is that, as your company scales up and your brand becomes increasingly prominent and profitable, you need to be increasingly proactive to police and monitor the integrity of your brand and take action, where necessary, to enforce your registered rights which are its legal foundation.

ENFORCEMENT: THE VOICE THAT IS FIRM AND ASSERTIVE

You are taking proactive measures to police your trademark rights as discussed in the previous paragraph. It follows therefore that you need to be prepared to maintain the competitive space around the legal monopoly you have obtained by virtue of your portfolio of trademark registrations. You need to be proactive in opposing conflicting marks, particularly in your key markets. Additionally and hopefully more rarely, you will need to enforce your rights through the courts if necessary. For that, you will need to allocate a litigation war chest each year to take on these conflicts.

As a rule of thumb an average business spends an estimated 10% of its revenue on all IP protection annually (including trademarks). However, that is not the end of the financial provision you should make; an additional 10–15% of that IP budget should be set aside for legal enforcement activity to cover the range of activity described above. This percentage will grow significantly if you happen to find yourself on the receiving end of a successful litigation.

Failure to enforce your legal rights leads ultimately to dilution of your brand and of course a negative impact to your business health and bottom line.

ENJOY THE JOURNEY: BRAND STRATEGY TO FOLLOW YOUR BUSINESS

The best brand strategies we have seen are those where there is a close cooperation and clear communication between the main stakeholders at the very outset. Discussing the brand values, understanding the company's vision and growth plans requires involving both the top decision-makers of the company as well as brand designers and IP practitioners. Only a strategy that takes into account and understands the perspectives of all parties will allow the creation of a brand that has a clear pathway to grow and support the business's aspirations. Additionally, engaging all the top stakeholders early on and getting their clear sign-off to establish default instructions will allow them to delegate and get on with the other tasks demanding their time.

In summary, as you scale up, a strong, well-protected brand is crucial to your business's success. There is a clear and direct causal link between repeat sales and increased profit margins to the strength of your brand, so it is well worth spending more time and allocating budget to get it right from the beginning rather than executing the trial-and-error strategy which ultimately often results in a bigger cost allocation.

1.4

GRANTS AND INCENTIVES WITHIN THE UK

Olaf Swanzy

INTRODUCTION

Despite current uncertainties surrounding the UK's relationship with the EU due to Brexit, there are numerous grant funding measures available to strengthen UK industry by stimulating growth, employment and the development of state-of-the-art technology which allows the UK to compete effectively in the global market. In particular, the UK grant landscape is extremely buoyant, with a regular supply of varied funding programmes which are beneficial over loan or equity investment as they are non-repayable and do not require the dilution of shareholdings.

Thousands of different grant schemes, worth well in excess of £5 billion each year, are available for UK companies in an attempt to encourage, amongst other things, innovation and economic development.

In general there are four types of public funding incentives available in the UK:

- **Grants** – where funding is secured ahead of the launch of a project;
- **Soft loans** – where loans are secured for projects that fall outside the parameters of normal business banking;

- **Tax incentives** – recognising advanced financial incentives for those with leading-edge Research and Development (R&D) or capital programmes that are aligned with government strategy;
- **Awards** – that retrospectively recognise industry excellence in many functional areas of business – usually a financial prize, which has the advantage of significant PR.

Outside of the obvious fiscal benefits, for successful applicants the receipt of public funding can be also be used to achieve the following:

- Increased project leverage and project development;
- Improved company image (being awarded a grant is the equivalent of being awarded a quality stamp from a grantor body);
- A competitive advantage over others in your sector;
- Help raising additional 'harder finance' – comparable investment criteria;
- Establishment of collaborative relationships. Not all grants require a collaboration, but those that do provide an ideal opportunity to work with academia, or indeed other industrial organisations, including potential customers.

In all cases, funding is used by a governmental body or policy maker to address key policy issues and to stimulate first movers by reducing financial risk in that area. Such incentives are therefore always in line with Government policies and key drivers. It is important that this is kept clearly in mind for any potential applicant when positioning their applications.

Although other forms of public funding are available, this article will focus predominantly on grants which represent the larger sums of money available for UK business.

MAIN GRANTS AND INCENTIVES IN THE UK

One of the key funding bodies to support UK businesses is Innovate UK (formerly the Technology Strategy Board), a fully public-funded executive body established in July 2007. Innovate UK is our national innovation agency, dedicated to driving innovation for wealth creation in the UK, so that technology-enabled businesses sustain or attain global significance. It provides particular support for Research and Development (R&D) to build partnerships between business, research and the Government to address major societal challenges and to run a wide range of knowledge exchange programmes to help innovation flourish. Funding is available for business and in some cases the academic base. The vision for Innovate UK is to make the UK a global leader in innovation and a magnet for innovative businesses, where technology is applied rapidly, effectively and sustainably to create wealth and enhance quality of life. Funding priorities are set each year in spring, communicated through an annual Delivery Plan. Further information can be found at www.gov.uk/government/organisations/innovate-uk.

Other sources of guidance and support for UK investment include: www.gov.uk/government/organisations/department-for-international-trade, www.scottish-enterprise.com, gov.wales/business-economy-innovation and www.investni.com.

In general, the range of funding programmes available for UK businesses can be broken down into the following three principal areas:

1. Research and Development;
2. Training and Education;
3. Capital Investment.

1. RESEARCH & DEVELOPMENT

Innovation remains the key focus area for the majority of UK funding bodies. A range of schemes are available for businesses irrespective of sector, company size and Technology Readiness Level (TRL). The core national funding programmes, designed to support businesses in their R&D activities, offer up to 70% grant funding for projects up to £1 million in cost. They have been summarised below.

For technical feasibility studies and industrial research, funding rates are:

- 70% for small businesses
- 60% for medium-sized businesses
- 50% for large businesses

For experimental development projects, the funding rates are:

- 45% for small businesses
- 35% for medium-sized businesses
- 25% for large businesses

Innovate UK Smart Funding (formerly the Open Programme)
Available for UK-based enterprises to support projects that aim to develop or demonstrate highly innovative processes, products or services that have the potential to deliver significant business growth. The competition, which is typically run across four calls per year, is open to all sectors and will support projects at different levels of

maturity, from initial ideas through to advanced prototype development. To be in scope, a proposal must show:

- Cutting-edge, disruptive or game-changing innovation leading to novel, new products, processes or services; and
- A clear and anticipated growth impact leading to a significant return on investment.

Manufacturing and Materials (Innovate UK)

This competition, which is also deployed typically across two calls per year, aims to stimulate and broaden innovation in manufacturing and materials, to increase productivity, competitiveness and growth for UK businesses, especially SMEs. To be in scope, a project must cover at least one of two areas:

- Innovation in a manufacturing system, technology, process or business model; e.g. more flexible or efficient processes and those that allow greater customisation of products;
- Innovation in materials development, properties, integration or reuse; e.g. materials for ease of manufacture or for targeted performance;
- Each project must focus on the manufacturing or materials innovation, rather than a product innovation – the challenge should be in the manufacturing process or materials development.

All projects must enable a step change in productivity and competitiveness for at least one UK SME. Applications are particularly welcome where the innovation can impact on more than one sector.

Emerging & Enabling Technologies (Innovate UK)

This scheme aims to identify and invest in new technologies coming from the research base that allow things to be done that were not previously possible (emerging) and the underpinning capabilities that improve existing industries (enabling). Proposals must show innovation in one of the key priority areas (see below), have outputs applicable to more than one market or sector, and improved business growth, productivity or export opportunities. Key priority areas include:

- Emerging technologies, including biofilms, energy harvesting, graphene or novel single-layer (2D) materials, cutting-edge imaging technologies, and unconventional new computational paradigms such as biological computing;

- Digital, where there is significant development in one or more of: machine learning and artificial intelligence (AI), cyber security, data analytics or 'big data', distributed ledger technology (such as blockchain), Internet of Things (IoT), immersive technology (such as virtual or augmented reality) and innovative services or applications employing new forms of connectivity, including 5G;
- Enabling capabilities, such as electronics, sensors and photonics (ESP), robotics and autonomous systems and creative industry technologies;
- Space applications with innovation in at least one of satellite communications, satellite navigation, or earth observation and environmental monitoring services.

Health and Life Sciences (Innovate UK)

This scheme aims to stimulate innovation in health and life sciences that significantly increases competitiveness and productivity with a particular focus on SMEs. Key priority areas include:

- Agricultural productivity: advanced and precision engineering, fighting agro-chemical and antimicrobial resistance, biotic and abiotic stress resilience, individualised livestock/aquaculture nutrition and healthcare, and novel genetics and breeding;
- Food quality and sustainability: authenticity and traceability, nutritional value, food safety, modern food manufacturing methods, new and smarter ingredients, protein development, and smarter packaging;
- Precision medicine: the development of tests and/or diagnostic tools to select the best treatment, care pathways and disease management regimes for patients, paediatrics and child health, stratification in primary care and the community, companion diagnostics, antimicrobial resistance and developing capabilities to enable precision medicine (e.g. informatics, imaging techniques and biosciences);
- Advanced therapies: increasing commercial capacity/ productivity to manufacture viral vectors for use in the development of clinical cell and gene therapies for the treatment of human disease and disorders;
- Preclinical technologies: innovative platforms for analysing, screening and optimising potential new medicines and novel in vitro and in vivo models that determine mechanism of action, efficacy or safety of potential new medicines;

- Biosciences: synthetic biology, computational systems biology, biological sample preparation technologies, cells, tissues and communities as bio-manufacturing platforms.

Infrastructure Systems (Innovate UK)

A scheme that aims to stimulate innovation in infrastructure systems that provide critical services to our economy, environment and society, across a range of sectors, including energy, transport and city/urban systems. Solutions can include technologies such as communications, digital, electronics, novel materials and sensors. Projects must meet one of the specific competition themes:

- 'Smart' infrastructure: smart, resilient and sustainable integrated infrastructure that adds intelligence to:

    o improve functionality, capacity, productivity, security or whole-life performance;
    o improve resilience and sustainability;
    o reduce the risk of failure;
    o reduce whole-life costs or environmental impact

- Energy systems: innovations in the ability to match energy supply and demand, which are smart systems solutions that integrate energy generation and demand at local, regional or national scales, and create significant improvements in value proposition, energy affordability, security and reduced carbon emissions;
- Nuclear fission: innovations that lead to major cost reductions, improved asset integrity and supply chain development for the UK and global civil nuclear markets, including decommissioning;
- Offshore wind: innovations that result in substantial reductions in the cost of energy from offshore wind;
- Connected transport: innovations that:

    o improve network capacity, efficiency and reduced operational cost, whilst (i) balancing transportation infrastructure peak demands, (ii) connecting different transport modes to provide better services, greater flexibility and reliability, and (iii) reducing logistics problems
    o offer greater system intelligence in existing transport networks
    o future-proof transport infrastructure for advanced vehicle technologies;

- Urban living: innovations that address citizens' challenges in cities and urban areas and offer citizen-centric solutions such as better health and wellbeing, increased productivity and higher resilience to change, by integrating different types of urban infrastructure systems.

Small Business Research Initiative (SBRI) (Innovate UK)

The SBRI supports the engagement of the public sector with industry during the early stages of development, supporting projects across a range of industry sectors through the stages of feasibility and prototyping. The initiative is particularly suitable for SMEs and early-stage businesses, as it provides them with vital funding for the critical stages of product development, and gives them a fast-track and simplified process for working with the public sector. Typically, funding available is £100,000 for a feasibility stage project and £1 million for a development stage project.

Latest Funding Opportunities

Under the Industrial Strategy Challenge Fund, smart sustainable packaging has been a focus. At the time of publication, calls for feasibility and demonstrator projects recently closed in mid-February 2020 with a further call for feasibility studies and industrial research open for application until 1st April 2020.

Full information regarding the status of all UK managed funding programmes can be found at Knowledge Transfer Network[1] and for current funding support available and at Innovate UK.[2]

EUREKA Eurostars (joint programme between more than 30 EUREKA member countries and the European Union)

This programme supports research-performing SMEs to develop market-orientated innovative products, processes and services in a transnational context, i.e. involving at least one other partner from another Eurostars country. It remains to be seen whether the UK will retain its EUREKA membership having left the EU. Any topic will be considered (with the exception of military applications). The main programme criteria are:

- Consortium leader is an R&D performing SME from a Eurostars country which includes the UK;
- Eurostars R&D performing SMEs contribution is 50% or more of the total project cost;

---

1. www.ktn-uk.co.uk/funding
2. www.innovateuk.ukri.org

- The consortium is well balanced (no single participant or country is responsible for more than 75%);
- The project duration is up to three years;
- Market introduction is within two years of the project's completion;

In the UK, only research-performing SMEs have been eligible for funding under Eurostars. UK academics/universities and large companies were welcome to participate in a Eurostars project, but funded their own participation from other sources. The same rules did not apply for other member states, so for any potential collaboration it was necessary to check the terms specific to that country. Up to 60% of eligible costs were supported to a maximum grant level of €360,000 per UK partner in a Eurostars project. Further information can be found at www.eurostars-eureka.eu/.

Horizon 2020 (H2020) – European Funding

At a European Level, H2020 is the largest European funding programme for research and innovation, with nearly €80 billion of funding available over seven years (2014 to 2020). Horizon 2020 is the financial instrument implementing the Innovation Union and a Europe 2020 flagship initiative aimed at securing Europe's global competitiveness. With the emphasis on excellent science, industrial leadership and tackling societal challenges, Horizon 2020's goal is to ensure Europe produces world-class science, removes barriers to innovation and makes it easier for the public and private sectors to work together in delivering innovation. Horizon 2020 is open to everyone and has a simpler structure than previous programmes – reducing red tape and time so that participants can focus on what is really important. This approach helps new projects to get off the ground quickly – and achieve results faster. Full details can be found at ec.europa.eu/programmes/horizon2020/.

There has been some general confusion around UK participation in Horizon 2020 due to ongoing Brexit negotiations. However, until the point of the UK departure in January 2020, the UK was still a member state and therefore eligible to fully participate in the programme. Now that the UK are in the transition period, having left the EU under the terms of the withdrawal agreement (and not no-deal), the status of UK in terms of research collaboration remains the same, i.e. UK participants can continue to submit and lead bids for funding under Horizon 2020 with some exceptions relating to security issues and financial instruments for SMEs until the end of the transition period in December 2020, which fortunately coincides with the end of the Horizon 2020 program, also December 2020. However, due to the general confusion around UK participation post-Brexit and, because consortia were unwilling to include UK members due to perceived risks associated with their participation due to Brexit, the rate of UK participation has inevitably decreased over the past 3 years. For the following EU framework programme (Horizon Europe) UK participation will depend on how the UK-EU negotiations progress; however, indications are that UK will be able to participate in some form, likely as an associate/third country. Horizon Europe will have an even stronger focus on supporting innovative SMEs compared to Horizon 2020, providing a wealth of opportunities for UK businesses.

2. TRAINING AND EDUCATION

The importance of training and upskilling employees is reflected in the wide-ranging government support available to businesses for staff development at all levels. This ranges from training for personnel below NVQ level 2 (secondary education), minority groups such as asylum seekers, to degree level, all through various mechanisms.

For example, apprenticeships are available to school leavers and provide on-the-job training in a wide variety of fields and sectors. Apprentices are assessed on an ongoing basis, leading to industry-recognised standards and qualifications at 4 levels and can include up to higher/degree level.

Innovate UK also offer Knowledge Transfer Partnerships (KTP), a scheme designed to help businesses in the UK innovate and grow, by linking them with an academic or research organisation and a graduate in a three-way knowledge-based partnership. This enables businesses to bring in new skills and access specialist academic research to achieve strategic innovation goals.

3. CAPITAL INVESTMENT

Few CAPEX support programmes remain in the UK, with a greater number of smaller schemes available at a regional/local level, depending on location. For larger-scale investments, the main national funding programme is the Regional Growth Fund (RGF). RGF is a £3.2 billion fund, helping companies throughout England to create jobs between now and the mid-2020s. The payment of RGF money is spread between 2011 and 2017. RGF supports projects and programmes that are using private sector investment to create economic growth and sustainable employment. The bid threshold (a minimum amount of funding that can be applied for) is £1 million. Any support will be phased in line with expenditure and/or job creation/safeguarding.

If you are considering an investment that will lead to job creation, it is worth speaking initially to your Local Enterprise Partnership about the availability of funding: www. gov.uk/government/policies/local-enterprise-partnerships-leps-and-enterprise-zones.

THE GRANT APPLICATION PROCESS

Thorough preparation is the key to success in applying for grants. Having a credible business plan, a clear commercial or marketing strategy as well as a quality management team, before an application is submitted, is a very important part of the application process. Application processing times differ significantly from scheme to scheme, with timescales ranging from four weeks to nine months. For potential applicants it is important that project costs are not incurred before the grant application process is completed and grant agreements signed with the appropriate funding body.

Careful preparation of applications will naturally increase the chances of success. However, there are no guarantees that an application will succeed, regardless of its merits, as the majority of UK grants are discretionary, meaning that they are awarded on a case-by-case basis and, more commonly, on a competitive basis. It is therefore of vital importance to ensure that the application is of the highest quality so that it stands out against the competition. It is also prudent to maximise the chances of success by developing a total grants strategy, rather than pinning everything on just one application.

SUPPORT IN THE GRANT ACQUISITION PROCESS

Finding the most appropriate grant and applying for funds can often be prohibitive. Successful grant procurement requires dedicated time and resources which companies often do not possess internally. As a result some businesses choose to maximise the funding opportunities available by appointing external expertise. Support advice and providers can be found through bodies such the UK Government Business Link network and the Enterprise Europe Network as well as specialist funding consultants. One such public funding advisory is the PNO Group – Europe's leading innovation funding advisors. Employing over 450 staff across the EU, PNO's core business is advising organisations across all industrial sectors, in the context of the UK and EU grant funding landscape, helping them to identify and secure funds through available schemes. For further information, please contact +44 (0) 161 488 3488 (tel) or visit the website: www.pnoconsultants.com/uk/.

CONCLUSION

Public funding can provide a valuable means of supporting companies to achieve their strategic goals. For R&D activities in particular there are a range of schemes available to support projects across all stages of development from initial conception through to large-scale demonstration.

With many businesses struggling to raise private and bank finance to advance their activities, it has never been more important to review all forms of funding available, including public funds. If you are serious about being a market leader in your field, grant funding is the ideal mechanism to help you to achieve your goal.

1.5

AN OVERVIEW OF THE UPDATED R&D TAX CLAIM REGIME

Mark Graves, Julia May, May Figures Ltd

The UK R&D tax credit Scheme is an extremely valuable source of R&D funding to companies; since its introduction in 2000–1 to 2017–18, over 300,000 claims have been made, with £26.9bn in tax relief claimed [1].

Now approaching its 20th year of operation, many readers will be aware of the basics of the scheme, most fundamentally that this tax relief provides either a corporation tax reduction (for profitable companies) or a cash rebate/increase in tax losses (for loss-making companies) based on allowable qualifying R&D expenditure. Allowable expenditure includes staff salary costs (wages, NIC and pensions), consumables used in the course of R&D (e.g. materials consumed in prototyping/experimentation, energy/water costs) and software license costs. Costs of external company's workers undertaking the R&D can also be claimed (usually at 65% of eligible costs), but there are detailed rules depending upon whether the company undertaking the R&D is considered a subcontractor or the provider of workers. This is a specific legislative distinction which can significantly affect the eligibility of such costs depending upon how the contractual arrangements between the claimant company and the external body undertaking the work.

What is less widely known is that there are in fact two distinct R&D tax credit schemes: (i) the SME scheme, which is only available to small and medium-sized companies; (ii) the RDEC scheme, which applies to larger companies or certain projects undertaken by SMEs. The tax relief under the SME scheme can be three times higher than that available under the RDEC scheme, so there are strict rules about qualification of the company and its particular project to restrict claims under the SME scheme to the most appropriate situations.

A stand-alone SME is defined as having less than 500 employees with either a turnover of less than 100 million euros or a balance sheet of less than 86 million euros. The rules are more restrictive for SMEs with LARGE shareholders or forming part of a group. One restriction application to the project itself (rather than the size of the claimant company) identifies projects that have been financed by clients or grants – these will not qualify for the SME scheme relief.

In this (and other) situations the SME company can claim under the RDEC scheme instead. This is a particularly complex area of R&D tax credits and we have previously written a book chapter explaining this in some detail [1].

This chapter provides an update of recent developments legislation, case law and HMRC guidance that have occurred since our last chapter in 2017.

R&D TAX CLAIM LEGISLATION UPDATES – SME CASH REBATE CAP FROM 1 APRIL 2020

The SME scheme can provide a cash rebate for companies who are loss-making for tax purposes either as a result of general trading, or because the R&D tax relief eliminates its taxable profit and creates a tax loss. On a spend of £100,000 on qualifying R&D activities, the refund could be as much as £33,350 – over a third back of the expenditure. Historically the cash refund was capped by reference to the company's PAYE/NIC liability, but this cap was removed in 2012.

As can be seen, the cash rebate is extremely valuable, especially for early-stage technology companies, and indeed many companies are even able to access short-term funding secured on their future R&D tax credit refunds, borrowing from specialist R&D loan bridging-loan finance providers as set out in another publication [3], accelerating the cash in-flow to the earliest possible time.

Unfortunately, the value has attracted a number of fraudulent claims. HMRC has identified and prevented fraudulent attempts to claim the SME scheme payable tax credit totalling over £300 million [4]. In these cases, companies were set up to claim the cash available through the payable tax credit even though they had no R&D activity at all and HMRC further identified structures set up primarily for the purpose of claiming the payable tax credit by means of re-routing the expenditure through a UK entity despite there being little (if any) employment or activity in the UK [4].

In the Autumn Budget 2018, in order to deter such abuse, it was announced that from 1 April 2020 (following legislation in the Finance Bill 2019–20), the amount of payable tax credit that a qualifying loss-making company can receive in any one year will be capped at three times the company's total PAYE and NICs liability for that year. Companies exceeding this cap on the refund would still have the option of claiming R&D tax relief, but they would have to retain the excess tax losses to be used in the usual ways (carry-forward/carry-back or group relief) and the cash refund would be limited.

HMRC acknowledged that such a cap would be detrimental to a number of early-stage technology start-ups who have a limited number of employees but who subcontract or outsource. Consequently, they administered a period of consultation which started on 28 March 2019 and closed on 24 May 2019. Specific areas that were considered were a threshold beyond which a cap was introduced, issues arising where a company was part of a group of companies or connected to another company and consideration of whether carried forward R&D tax losses could be surrendered in a time period (of say two years) if a company had by then generated sufficient PAYE and NIC liability [4].

The result of this consultation was not reported at the time other Finance Bill consultations were reported on 11 July 2019, and so at the time of writing this chapter it is not certain whether there will be any amendments to the originally proposed legislation.

Despite this uncertainty there are a number of measures that loss-making technology firms should be considering. These include:

- bringing externally provisioned R&D in-house to be conducted by employees. This would also remove the 65% restriction on subcontractors/externally provided workers.
- changing the company year end to be able to make another claim before the new rules commence. The new rules apply to the first accounting period commencing after 1 April 2020. There are however anti-avoidance rules as to when and for what purpose a company can shorten its year end, and hence companies should seek professional advice from a regulated advisor (Chartered Accountant/Chartered Tax Advisor) rather than rely on advice from the growing band of unregulated R&D tax credit advisors, many of whom have no training, qualifications or professional indemnity insurance covering taxation advice.

CASE LAW UPDATE – TEKSOLUTIONS INC. – RECORD KEEPING

The main case law update during this period was Teksolutions Inc. v HMRC, held at the First-Tier Tribunal Tax Chamber in Birmingham on 16th September 2019 and published on 7th November 2019. The company claimed that it has incurred the expenditure related to 3 R&D projects on its work on nozzles, PPMA/graphene and polymers.

HMRC's case was that the expenses claimed in the R&D analysis and the tax returns did not correlate in any meaningful way. HMRC was unclear as to the extent that the expenditure said to have been incurred in relation to the three projects had already been included in the expenses claimed in the tax returns and accounts and that the Appellant had failed to provide documentary evidence to support the claimed expenditure.

During the hearing the Appellant argued that they could not have conducted the extensive research that it had (research was evidenced by the project summaries and slide show document produced by the Appellant) without incurring the claimed expenditure.

The Tribunal confirmed that the Law as defined in Schedule 18 of the Finance Act 1998 provides that a company must keep such records as may be needed to enable it to deliver a correct and complete return and preserve those records until the sixth anniversary of the end of the period for which the company may be required to deliver a company tax return, and that an office of HMRC may enquire into an amended company tax return if they give notice of an intention to do so by the 21st January, 30th April, 31st July or 31st October next following the first anniversary of the day on which the amendment was made.

The Tribunal ruled in favour of HMRC and further imposed a penalty of £25,791.21 on the Appellant.

The key point of highlighting this particular case is that claimants need to have thorough documentation to demonstrate that the expenses being claimed on the various R&D projects are properly supported with receipts, correctly and have been paid at the time of applying for the R&D tax credit.

It has been common practice for estimates to be used when preparing claims, for staff allocation of time, heat and light and materials consumed in the R&D projects. These are now areas on which to focus and upgrade or put in place detailed record keeping supporting a robust, defensible claim.

HMRC GUIDANCE UPDATE – SOFTWARE CIRD81960

The most significant HMRC Guidance update is in the field of Software claims, with an update in October 2018 to their CIRD81960 guidance note 'R&D tax relief: conditions to be satisfied: BIS Guidelines – application to software', which had previously been produced in 2004 [5].

Still drawing on the over-arching Department for Business, Innovation and Skills (BEIS) Guidelines on the Meaning of Research and Development for Tax Purposes (CIRD81900) the purpose of this additional Guidance is to apply the concepts of scientific or technological advances, technological uncertainties and project boundaries to software projects. This guidance does not change the BEIS Guidelines but is intended to link scenarios common within the software sector to address common questions relating to software projects.

The fundamental requirements for a claim (the advance, the technological uncertainty and the boundaries of the R&D) have not changed but this updated guidance reflects HMRC's growing frustration that many claimants (especially those advised by generalist accountants or non-software specialist R&D claims advisors) fail to properly address these fundamentals properly when filing software claims.

'A claim which stated the advance as being in a certain area or field of software is not specific enough, if the advance sought is in a specific sub-area such as robotic process automation, augmented reality, microservices etc. The competent professional for the company's R&D project should be able to explain how the company's R&D project is new in, or an appreciable improvement to, that field of science or technology relative to that which is available in the public domain or was readily deducible.' [5]

HMRC inspectors have been supported by HMRC's internal computer specialists for some time now to ensure that their knowledge of this industry is kept updated and their computer specialists provide advice based on their knowledge of particular software packages and applications. This enables Inspectors to ask more pertinent questions directly relevant to the software advance. These replace the generalist questions such as:

'What is the baseline in technology that any advance sought is being measured against?' or 'Is it the underlying technology in which an advance is being made rather than the commercial output or outcome?' [5]

The new guidance gives an example of how an advanced or appreciable improvement can be identified by measuring and comparing it to a comparable family (or category) of software that is viewed as representing the current state of overall capability in that area (proprietary or open source software frameworks).

Academic literature baseline

One key takeaway is that it is not acceptable to submit a software claim just listing the 'features and benefits' of the new software code that was developed (in fact, it never was) – instead the software development needs to be described in the context of how it advances the field of software in which it resides – this can only be done by a rigorous academic literature review summarising the baseline of the technological field at the start of the project. For our claims we have for several years supported our client's software claims with an academic literature review demonstrating the work as R&D and suspect that other leading advisors will adopt this practice as they face more direct inquiries.

A previously qualifying project may no longer be qualifying

HMRC describe how it can be sometimes be difficult to determine whether an advance is in the overall knowledge or capability (rather than a company's own) in such a fast-moving sector. *'R&D projects which were seeking such advances in previous years and were considered to meet the definition within the BEIS Guidelines **may not qualify now because technological capability has increased over time**, with solutions to what were previously technological uncertainties becoming available, or readily deducible, as the software industry moves forward to address new ideas.'* [5]

A project may have only be partially qualifying

*'The words "research and development" are frequently used within the software sector and care should be taken to assume that a commercial project fully aligns with the definition of R&D set out in the BEIS Guidelines. It may do, but in order to be included as a qualifying R&D project for the purpose of tax reliefs, **only those parts of the commercial project that meet the criteria** that are described in the BEIS Guidelines at CIRD81900 will be qualifying.'* [5]

The Guidance goes into much greater detail about when different elements of the software development process can/cannot be claimed (requirements gathering, planning, analysis, design and development, testing, non-functional testing, functional testing, deployment and maintenance) and consequently having an advisor who has a strong software development background and understands the full software development lifecycle is invaluable.

CONCLUSIONS

The cash rebate cap on SME claims after 1 April 2020 means that many companies that outsource a large proportion of their R&D may not receive a similar level of cash rebate that they have previously received or would otherwise be expecting. It is not too late to undertake careful analysis and planning of the organisation, its contracts and accounting periods to mitigate the effects.

Recent case law reiterates the need to have thorough record keeping in place in order to be able to defend an HMRC enquiry both to uphold the value of the claim and to avoid financial and reputationally costly penalties.

Software claims have always presented industry-specific challenges but the updated guidance and documented availability of the use of HMRC in-house software experts can be interpreted as a statement of intent by HMRC to investigate more claims in this field and so the need for preparing robust claims clearly articulating the baseline technology (ideally a thorough academic prior art literature review), how the development advances the baseline technology, the technological uncertainties, the project boundaries and understanding and justification for each of the software development tasks has become increasingly important.

REFERENCES

1. 'R&D Tax Credits – Totally Brilliant – but Not Just a Walk in the Park' by Terry Toms in *Growing Business Innovation – Developing, Promoting and Protecting IP*, edited by Jonathan Reuvid, Legend Press, 2019.
2. 'R&D Tax Credit Claims – an Overview of the SME and LARGE/ RDEC Schemes' by Mark Graves and Julia May in *Growing Business Innovation – Developing, Promoting and Protecting IP*, edited by Jonathan Reuvid, Legend Press, 2019.
3. 'R&D Tax Credit Claim-Based Short-Term Bridge Finances for High-Tech Start-ups' by Mark Graves and Julia May in *Growing Business Innovation – Developing, Promoting and Protecting IP*, edited by Jonathan Reuvid, Legend Press, 2019.
4. 'Preventing Abuse of the R&D Tax Relief for SMEs: consultation', HM Treasury and HM Revenue & Customs, www.gov.uk/government/consultations/preventing-abuse-of-the-rd-tax-relief-for-smes.
5. 'R&D Tax Relief: Conditions to Be Satisfied: BIS Guidelines (formerly DTI Guidelines) (2004) – Application to Software', HM Revenue & Customs, www.gov.uk/hmrc-internal-manuals/ corporate-intangibles-research-and-development-manual/ cird81960

1.6

R&D TAX CREDITS – TOTALLY BRILLIANT – BUT NOT JUST A WALK IN THE PARK

Terry Toms, RandDTax

THE BIG PICTURE – CONTRIBUTING TO INNOVATION

The latest figures on R&D claims were published by The Office for National Statistics (ONS) on 10th October 2019. They cover 2017–2018 and due to the backwards looking nature of R&D claims, companies can claim within two years of an accounting period end for that period, will understate the numbers.

Headlines 2017–2018

- £4.3 billion of tax relief support estimated to rise to $5 billion. (Final Revised figure for 2016–2017 £4.4 billion)
- 42,705 SME R&D claims. (Final Revised figure for 2016–2017 45,045)
- For the largely final 2016–17 figures 23% of claimants were first time.
- Over 300,000 claims since the two scheme began.
- £26.9 billion in relief since the two scheme began.
- Final figures for 2017–18 expected to reach almost £5 billion. This means almost 1/5 of the amount claimed in 18 years will be in that one year.

- 2016–17 figures are much more finalised than 2017–2018. They showed 23% of claimants were first time.
- 25% of claims were 'Manufacturing', 24% 'Information and Communication', and 20% 'Professional, Scientific and Technical'.
- Can the other 31%? 'Wholesale & Retail Trade, Repairs', 'Financial & Insurance', 'Admin & Support Services', 'Mining & quarrying', 'Arts, Entertainment and Recreation' are the larger components.
- Software development likely to be underrepresented in 'Information & Communication' because Software is likely to be in a lot of areas, as they rank on the companies area of activity not the nature of the R&D claim.

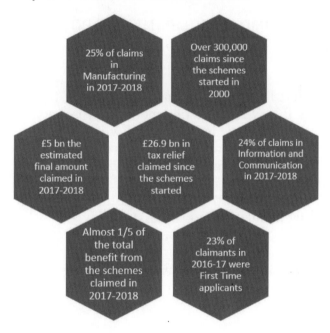

So, what is the trend?

A straight reading suggests a fall in claims and support. However, claims for years ending up to March 2018 are still being made. We are making them this month and will continue to make claims for years ending in that period until 31st March 2020. So, the important numbers for comparison are the original 2016–2017 numbers.

2016–2017 Published in September 2018
£3.5 billion in tax relief support
34,060 SME R&D Claims
Conclusion
SME Claims up by roughly 25%

So, like for like at the same point in the reporting cycle the amount of support is up by almost 23% and the number of claims is up 25%. Remember we are looking back, but as of 2017–2018 it is hard to see any fall back in R&D claim activity, just huge growth.

To estimate forward: it is likely by this time next year we could see a more complete level of support at £5.4 billion with something like 56,000 SME claims for 2017–18, extrapolating this from the previous rise in 2016–2017 the numbers. This is great news for the government, which have put R&D at the forefront of post-Brexit economic policy as SMEs drive a large part of the UK economy.

Our experience suggests that many companies are still missing out on this vital funding by not claiming or underclaiming.

ANY TYPE OF LIMITED COMPANY CAN POTENTIALLY CLAIM R&D TAX CREDITS

We are often asked the question: What types of companies qualify for R&D tax credits? The short answer is that any type of company **could** qualify if they are investing money and/or time in attempting to enhance either knowledge or capability in an area of science or technology, or in other words, innovating in the way they operate their business – finding better ways to do things. The innovation could result in an attempt to develop a new or improved product, process, service, material or device. Figure 1.6.1 below illustrates some of the types of companies that RandD Tax has successfully advised.

Figure 1.6.1 – Small selection of company types advised by RandD Tax

Application software developers

Brewers   Manufacturers

Test and Calibration companies

Legal Firms   **Bailiffs**

Refurbishing of industrial components   Software tool developers

Manufacturers of machinery

Engineering companies   Security Systems Software

Ice Cream   IT infrastructure

Injection Moulding   Designer and manufacturer of industrial components

Winch makers   Motor Industry

Industrial process control systems

Financial Services Companies

This picture is by no means comprehensive, but it illustrates the variety. The two very obvious sectors cover all the massive variety of manufacturing, science and technology-based businesses while the less obvious are professional services companies of all types including architects, consulting and environmental engineers and even bailiffs. Information technology-based systems have the potential to totally transform the way companies and whole industries operate, while sometimes less obvious science and technology-based activities can transform more mundane activities such as packaging or extending the quality shelf life of food products. In engineering, all good companies innovate – and more broadly ALL companies attempt to innovate. It is astonishing, therefore, that the number of SMEs claiming is still only around 1%. I talked to one very small client this week who has just been chosen as the only authorised supplier in a niche engineering sector by the largest food manufacturer in the world because of the innovative technology they have developed over the last five years; and he talked about the importance of R&D tax credits in funding the work to achieve this status. I could fill endless articles with such case studies, and in this and very many examples they did not realise that they might qualify simply because they are very busy just doing what they do.

We often take on new clients who have either claimed on their own, aided by their tax accountants or have used other advisers. We provide a free audit of previous claims where we are still in time to correct omissions. More often than not we will find blind spots, some very significant, where the company has not recognised work they do as qualifying R&D. It is not only vital that companies understand the HMRC guidelines related to claims. They whould understand how those are applied in their own industry sector.

BUT NOT JUST A WALK IN THE PARK

In the UK our tax systems virtually all operate on a self-assessment basis, much along the lines of HMRC giving taxpayers enough rope to hang themselves. We will often talk with companies and even their accountants, who will say things like 'we/our client have/has claimed R&D tax credits successfully for the last six years or more years'. Then HMRC decide to ask a few simple questions related to the latest claim or an older one, and before you know it an official tax enquiry has been triggered. Where HMRC identify invalid overclaiming, they have almost unlimited power to investigate claims from current and previous years; and penalties can be incurred as well as overpayments repaid. While this process may seem unfair to some companies it is very difficult to see how HMRC could handle compliance in a better or more cost-effective manner. As taxpayers, none of us want to see companies gaining cash from our tax system that they are simply not entitled to claim. Overclaiming on R&D tax credit claims is certainly NOT a victimless crime. Our advice to Directors of claiming companies is to ensure that they fully understand the HMRC guidelines, how these are applied in their sector and that they can sleep at night with the claim values submitted. Sadly, we see increasing evidence that advisers do not ask enough questions, publish wide-reaching disclaimers and often turn a blind eye to abuse of the R&D tax credit schemes.

ON THE OTHER HAND THERE CAN BE MANY REASONS THAT YOU ARE NOT GETTING ALL YOU DESERVE

What are some of these reasons?

- It may be that you do not accurately recognise that you are doing qualifying R&D.
- Even where you do recognise that you are doing R&D, you and your advisors may not fully appreciate all the areas in your business where technically qualifying R&D work begins and ends.
- You may be paying too high a share of the R&D Tax benefits gained in advisors' fees.
- You may be spending too much time and cost on the claims process.
- You may have made a claim or claims that HMRC have questioned, rejected or reduced, and you have lost confidence in the claims process, or are facing HMRC enquiries.
- You may have set up sales or procurement processes which can make claiming full R&D tax credits either difficult or impossible.

THE SMALLER PICTURE

When we started RandDTax in 2012 our aim was to create a business model which delivered outstanding value through an innovative structure and business processes. In December 2017 we were successful in winning the Business Innovation Award, part of the National SME Awards. The judges said, 'Here is a business that is self-assured and unexpectedly using innovation to its great advantage.' I did not entirely agree with the 'self-assured' comment and thought that the 'unexpectedly using innovation' statement probably referred to the mass of grey and disappearing hair on the heads of our founding team. Innovation is often seen as a young person's game. However, advancing age has been very advantageous for many unexpected reasons, not least of which is the outstanding pool of talent represented by our founders' offspring, in the breeding and training of a new generation of consultants. We are now a family business but not limited to one family. RandDTax now has 19 shareholders, all of whom are either consultants or in key operational roles. The combination of our very interesting and innovative client base plus good consultants has made RandDTax a very interesting business. Our belief is that this has enabled us to deliver exceptional value to clients in an R&D consultancy market which has become very crowded and variable in quality of service.

Given the growth in the number of claims being made, we operate in a market which is seen as growing fast. Our growth as a company has been consistent, all claims have been successful and almost all of our clients were introduced to us by their accountants or by other RandDTax clients. It can be hard for companies to select consultancy partners in this space, and it is very tempting for both claiming companies and their advisers to cut corners in the claim process. We do not feel that printed disclaimers are any substitute for doing everything possible to ensure claims are valid when submitted, in order to protect our clients. The result for RandDTax has been a very low level of questions from HMRC related to claims. In advising on well in excess of 5,000 claims for over 1,200 clients over the last 7 years, questions have been asked by HMRC in less than 0.5% of cases.

Our clients have benefitted by an average of around £103,000 each and we have operated for seven years. This means that we could have advised clients on at least 1 but up to 7 or more claims. The HMRC/National Audit Office figures suggest that annual claims are worth an average of around £50,000, although much smaller sums of money are often vital to the survival of young innovative technology companies; so our 'war stories' include numerous situations where first meetings took place in humble front rooms or converted garages, and those young companies have since progressed to relative stardom – and the award of R&D tax credits has made a significant contribution to that success. If you are interested in looking into this aspect of R&D tax credits in greater detail, we have published a White Paper in the Blog section of our web site. This was the output of an MBA research project by one of our Directors/Shareholders. The title is 'Research and Development Tax Relief for UK SMEs – a Good Thing?' and the author is Tim Walsh BSc, MBA, CTA. At the time the work on this was carried out Tim could find no existing study related to R&D tax relief which focused exclusively on SMEs.

BACK TO THE BIG PICTURE

There are well in excess of 4.5 million SME companies in the UK. I find it hard to believe that less than 0.5% of SMEs are investing in trying to developing the capabilities of science or technology to produce better products, enhanced services, more efficient processes, more powerful devices or much better materials. We see the brilliant results of UK R&D in every way, every day of our lives.

All companies want to gain real competitive advantage with new or enhanced products, services, processes, devices and materials. Advances in science and technology provide the ideal platform for this as we enter the Fourth Industrial Revolution (4IR), and that should be the main topic for our politicians to bang on about, when and if the dust ever settles one way or another on Brexit. Real industrial and economic strength comes from constantly striving for meaningful innovation – finding much better ways of doing stuff – and I find that SMEs in the UK are truly inspirational in applying, adapting and developing in areas of science and technology.

PART TWO
PREPARING
TO EXPORT

2.1

VERIFYING THAT PATENTS REMAIN IN FORCE

Margit Hoehne, patentGate

LEGAL STATUS OF PATENTS

One interesting fact about patents is the contrast between legal and technical aspects of those intellectual property rights. While the content of a patent document describes the novelty and ingenuity of a technical innovation, and the claims translate the invention into comparable and enforceable legal terms, there are life phases and events that have a large impact on the legal validity of the patent.

These legal events determine if a patent is still 'alive' or is not any longer in force. Knowing this impacts questions like: Is the invention considered state of the art and can be used without infringing any patent? Can this invention be used freely or is it necessary to license it? Has the assignee declared his willingness to grant a licence?

INTRODUCTION

A legal event is data concerning the life cycle of a patent or other intellectual property right like trademarks or designs.

They describe the steps beginning with the filing at a patent office to the end of the IP right's life. This event history shows all events and the legal status, which describes whether an IP right is still in force. It is maintained within the patent register of the filing office.

The part of the patent register that is accessible by the public contains only events for IP rights that have already been published.

A patent application will be published 18 months after filing by the patent office. If a priority is claimed within 12 months, the first publication occurs 18 months after the priority date, which is the filing date of the first filing at another patent office for this application.

The event of filing and all others that take place until the patent application has been published will not be known to the public before the publication day. They are, however, already stored in a section of the patent register that is not open to the public. When the IP right is published, all events up to that time will be available in the patent register.

Some events may occur before or after the publication, for instance the request for examination. Others, like claiming a foreign priority, take place before publication.

There are differences between legal status and legal events. The status describes in one phrase if a IP right is still in force or not at the current date. To every patent application there is a list of legal events. These can either be neutral, positive or negative.

An example for a neutral event could be the communication with the examining division. This can only be interpreted when the content of the examination report is considered.

Positive events, that indicate the IP right is still in force, are the payment of the annual fee or the request for examination. Other events like filing for opposition or the decision to reject indicate that the patent could be lapsed.

Most IP offices publish a weekly gazette on paper or online that lists all publications, grants, corrections, as well as legal events and changes in legal status for that week. The patent register contains all information for all IP rights at a given time. The selection of events and how detailed they are published in the register and/or gazette can differ.

The register differentiates between the date of the procedural status and the date of publication in the patent register or patent gazette.

While the date of the procedural status is the day when the event has occurred, the public will be informed about it later on the date of publication in the register or gazette.

Sometimes an event's legal effect will not occur, for instance when a missed fee payment has been rectified within a defined deadline. That means that you can not determine with only the occurrence of a legal event if an IP right is still in force or not. It is in force while the legal status in the register is still 'in force' or 'pending'.

Some patent offices provide in the legal status if a patent is not in force anymore. The British Intellectual Property Office indicates if a patent is 'Expired', the German Patent and Trademark Office declares it

'Not pending / Lapsed'. The European Patent Office (EPO) publishes no such information in the register, but has 14 different legal status values.

Table 2.1.1 – Status values for European Patents

Indicator	Legal status
IP right in force	Examination is in progress
	Grant of patent is intended
	Opposition filed
	Request for examination was made
	The application has been published
	The patent has been granted
IP right not in force	Patent revoked
	The application has been refused
	The application has been withdrawn
	The application is deemed to be withdrawn
Granted EP patents	No opposition filed within time limit
	Opposition procedure closed
	Opposition rejected
	Patent maintained as amended

The legal status for granted EP patents is not found at a single source, because after grant and the entry in the national phases the information can be found in the registers of the designated contracting states, validation states and extension states. It can be in force as long as it is still valid in at least one of those states. With the implementation of the Federated Register it has become easier to collect the legal status for all countries concerned.

The following chapters introduce public services of patent offices for legal status information: INPADOC, the largest worldwide legal status database; the Global Dossier, a service of the five largest IP offices and EPO's Federated register with data for the national phase of European patents.

INPADOC LEGAL STATUS DATABASE PROVIDED BY THE EPO

INPADOC is the largest worldwide legal status database. It is maintained by the European Patent office and contains more than 275 million legal events.

The EPO publishes weekly statistics that show the growth of the data and which countries are covered.

An evaluation of the data of week 20/2019 shows that those 275 million legal events are related to 56 million patent applications from 52 countries. They are classified with 3,900 legal event codes.

The biggest portion is data from the EPO with more than 80 million events, the IP offices of Japan, China, USA, Korea, Germany and the World Intellectual Property Organisation WIPO provided more than 10 million events each to the EPO.

The events represented in the INPADOC database are sometimes not as much detailed like in the register of the national IP office. The update frequency and completeness of the data is not the same for all offices.

Sometimes similar events will be grouped together in one event code or are not represented in INPADOC at all. The time lag between the occurrence of the event and the publication in INPADOC can be weeks or even months.

The average number of events per document in the database is four, EP publications have a higher average of 23 events. The data is updated weekly.

INPADOC data is provided in Espacenet as 'INPADOC legal status' and is used by commercial patent information providers for their own databases.

The legal status of a patent family can be obtained easily in Espacenet because all documents of a patent family are displayed there.

WIPO PATENTSCOPE

Patentscope is a service of World Intellectual Property Organisation (WIPO). The database contains mainly bibliographic data from the WIPO itself and 58 other countries worldwide, but also legal status information (displayed in the tabs 'National Phase' and 'Documents'). There is no link between members of a patent family.

To get an overview of all legal events of a patent family, using other services to find the patent family members is necessary.

For applications filed under the Patent Cooperation Treaty (PCT) the WIPO provides the documents from the search and examination procedure as well as related documents in the file inspection. WIPO provides a statistics table on their website with information how many national phase entries in which time frame are available in the Patentscope database.[1]

WIPO also provides a patent register portal on their website where databases, registers and online gazettes of more than 200 IP offices can be accessed.[2]

---

1. patentscope.wipo.int/search/en/nationalphase.jsf
2. www.wipo.int/patent_register_portal/en/index.html

This service can be used to find information about the content of national and regional registers.

GLOBAL DOSSIER

Patent documents published by an IP5 Office can be accessed via the Global Dossier. This is a joint project of the five largest IP offices to facilitate the access to the file wrappers of IP5 patent family members.

The IP5 member offices are

- European Patent Office (EPA)
- Japan Patent Office (JPO)
- Korean Intellectual Property Office (KIPO)
- National Intellectual Property Administration of the People's Republic of China (CNIPA)
- United States Patent and Trademark Office (USPTO)

The table shows the data coverage of the Global Dossier.

Table 2.1.2 – Global Dossier Coverage; Source: 'IP5 Global Dossier: Scope, Content, Availability and Performance'[3]

Patent office	Dossier type	Date range	Language
EPA	EP and PCT applications	All (from 1977)	Original EN/DE/FR
JPO	JP and PCT applications and utility models	application date from 01.07.2003	JP / EN (JPO machine translation)
KIPO	KR and PCT applications and utility models	application date from 01.01.1999	KR / EN (KIPO machine translation)
CNIPA	CN and PCT applications (no utility models)	application date from 10.02.2010	CN / EN (CNIPA machine translation)
USPTO	US and PCT applications	application date from 01.01.2003	EN
WIPO*	PCT applications	All (from 1978)	PCT publication languages
CIPO*	applications	Anmeldungen mit Prüfbericht ab 01.08.2015	Original EN/FR

* While WIPO and the Canadian Intellectual Property Office (CIPO) are not members of IP5, they provide data to the Global Dossier.

---

3. www.fiveipoffices.org/activities/globaldossier/filewrapper

The content of the Global Dossier is nearly identical to the online file wrappers at the IP5 office. When no document exists for a legal events, for instance fee payments, there is no entry of the event in the dossier.

Cited non-patent literature is not provided in the Global Dossier due to copyright issues.

The global dossier service can be accessed via the website of any IP5 office. The layout and language of the user interface differs, but the content is the same. For publications from China, Korea and Japan machine translations to English are provided parallel to the original document.

The number of daily requests can be limited by the office and some offices may have maintenance times where the server will be unavailable. The delay until a document is available within Global Dossier can be up to 8 weeks.

FEDERATED REGISTER

The Federated Register is a part of the European Patent Register and shows the consolidated status of the legal status of a granted European patent at the national offices of the designated states.

When an European patent has been granted, the tab 'Federated Register' can be accessed in the European Patent Register.

34 of the 38 member states of the European Patent Convention (EPC) provide deep links into their national patent registers, so that a patent's data is directly accessible. 29 office provide data to the EPO that is made available in the Federated Register. More offices will follow. Not all member states make their data available in the Federated Register. Denmark, France and Italy only supply links to their national register database: (Source: Federated Register – integration status 02/2019)[4]

For each patent the Federated register contains

- the link to the national register
- the legal status
- the application and publication number
- the applicant or proprietor
- the invalidation date
- the information since when the patent is not in force
- the last payment of renewal fees
- the date the record was last updated

---

4. www.epo.org/searching-for-patents/legal/register/documentation/data-coverage.html

for all designated contracting states, extension states and validation states that provide the data to the register. The list of states can differ for each EP patent.

Not all offices supply all the data in the table, but the EPO has documented the available coverage. For example the data provided by the German Patent Office (DPMA) are the legal status, application and publication number, proprietor and update date.

Even with the message '*No data provided by the national patent office for this patent*' there may be data in the national register.

The help page describes the 18 status values and their definition.

The links to the national patent registers at the bottom of the Federated Register page are the same as in the table above, when the office is listed in both sections.

If the Unitary Patent will enter into force, it will be possible to get combined patent protection in 26 EU member states by requesting unitary effect with the EPO. This will affect the data provided in the Federated register.

CONCLUSION

There are different sources for an IP right's legal status information: patent registers maintained by the filing office and secondary sources like the INPADOC database or the Global Dossier and Federated register, that provide consolidated information from different sources.

The completeness, accuracy and timeliness of these sources may vary, so legal status information should be interpreted with care. Patent attorneys and patent information professionals who have in-depth knowledge of the patent system and the available data sources can help interpret the legal status of patents.

2.2

STARTING OUT IN EXPORTING

Marcus Dolman and Susan Ross,
BExA British Exporters Association

Department for International Trade (DIT) research suggests around a third of exporters begin exporting in response to customer demand, many working through social or family ties. Exporting involves several layers of complexity that sit above domestic trade, and therefore needs to be managed proactively and accurately. In any case, even if a business begins exporting by chance, it must be with the intention that exporting will become a profit contributor, and to achieve this, it is helpful to develop an export strategy. This strategy should identify where it is easiest to do business, culturally and linguistically, and which markets offer the best sales opportunities.

The key question is, how do you get started? What kind of selling mode should you use? Which are the best countries to start in? How do you get your goods there? What information do you need to make the sale? Who is going to do each task?

Textbook marketing theory talks about entry modes. In simple terms, that means the method of selling goods or services, and how the business should be organised to do it. The choice revolves around three issues:

1. Business risk taken by exporter
2. Exporter's management control and visibility of the destination market
3. Flexibility

The good news is that you can be an arm's-length exporter – by selling through a trader, manufacturer or consolidator that has experience and existing trading patterns with the destination. However, by involving an intermediary, you are giving away margin, but then you are also insulating yourself from the inevitable extra risks of getting the goods to their destination, physical loss or damage, export and import customs duties, currency, overseas regulation, law and jurisdiction, and export payment risk.

Direct exporters who want to have a regular flow of sales tend to have representation in the destination country. This ranges from having an overseas agent working on your behalf, or appointing a distributor or dealer that resells your product under your brand, through to establishing an office or joint venture partner abroad.

Each route has its place, but the resources available to exploit the market and the level of risk the seller is prepared to take will determine which is most appropriate in the circumstances. For example, the sheer size and strategic potential of China may suggest a direct investment, whereas Zambia would suggest a distributor method. A very small market like Ascension may best be served by exporting directly from head office.

A good place to start for help and information is with DIT. This government-funded agency supports UK exporters and helps companies realise their international business potential through knowledge transfer and ongoing support. The DIT and Exporting is GREAT websites contain country information and details of the services on offer. 'Open to Export' has useful resources and pointers and you can submit questions to a panel of experts.

START WITH A PROFITABLE PRODUCT LINE

It is very difficult to start your first business with exporting. However, if you have a successful product in your home market, exporting can help you to grow and diversify. So, if you have a product that sells well here and is successful and profitable, you can understand its ins and outs and what works and doesn't work in the UK before going overseas. If your UK domestic business doesn't enjoy good margins, do not assume that, by adding export markets, you can improve your company's finances. It is only worth venturing overseas if the product is already profitable: exporting is going to take a lot of your time and is likely to cut into your margins. The cost of every aspect of business is higher, and your overseas representative will also want a percentage of sales.

BEGIN CLOSE TO HOME

With exporting, you need to take one step at a time: don't try to launch in every market. The nearest market to the UK is Ireland: they speak the same language, use the euro, and have strong ties with the UK.

If your product works in Ireland, look to countries with a similar customer profile, needs and wants. This may be to larger English speaking countries such as the USA or Canada, or closer to home into Europe. Benelux countries are physically close, speak English, and their population of 29m (under half that of the UK[1]) belies their trading skills. The Netherlands has its own industrial and agricultural exports and also acts as a distribution centre for continental Europe and is the world's eighth largest exporter, exporting four times as much per head of population as the UK.

> Notwithstanding this, one exporter writes, 'Export strategies for new exporters often suggest concentrate on easy, near markets. Sensible strategy, but in practice a good order from Japan is worth two promises from Ireland'.

Once your target list of destinations is established, start with the ones that you can get to easily on low-cost direct flights: your time is precious.

DEVELOPING YOUR PRODUCT FOR EXPORT

Look at what adaptations your product will need for your chosen export market. Is your product right? Get to know the competition. Look at the customer requirements. Try to imagine the position of the customer, the wholesaler and the retailer. What do they want? You are going to make a big investment in exporting, you need to protect your brand and provide good quality and service to encourage your customers to choose your product instead of their familiar locally produced product. You cannot afford to get it wrong.

> To enter the Japanese market, a consumer engineering company needed to design a tiny machine that could be put away in a cupboard in a typical Japanese home. Subsequently, the company discovered that customers in Europe also wanted a tiny machine.

Consider your Intellectual Property Rights, and be careful about which entities you license to distribute your products, for which sectors or

---

1. CIA World Fact Book

geography, and if exclusive or not. You do not want to have a licensee that has acted as a 'brand collector' and is not working hard enough for you. The *BExA Guide to Export Compliance*[2] has a useful checklist on this subject.

RESEARCH

Make sure you have time to spend on researching the market properly. Understand the culture and demographics of the country. Find out what sells locally, what price it is and what its shortcomings are. Understand what will be the best way to promote/market/advertise your product. Who are the key players? What can you learn from them? Taking a key UK customer out to your golf club might be a pleasant way to spend an afternoon and initiate some useful discussion, but it won't necessarily suit a French customer where golf is less popular, and instead an activity that demonstrates your appreciation of France's fine food could result in a stronger relationship.

Perfecting the image

A young electronics company had developed a calibration system to enable installers of digital TV to achieve the best reception. Exports were mainly to the USA and comprised 10% of turnover. An approach was made to DIT for advice about growing exports. The recommended strategy included being more proactive in seeking out new opportunities, using on-the-ground market information from overseas embassies who also supplied useful leads, and understanding the technology and consumer needs of each market before visits were made. New European markets were established and exports grew to 70–80% of turnover.

There is a lot of information on the internet, but the key is its interpretation. Ensure the data obtained is pertinent to the question. For example, some countries' economic and demographic information may be controlled by their governments. It may have been produced to toe the party line, may be misleading, inaccurate or even blatantly untrue.

If you are selling consumer products, information such as GNP and GDP are useful for identifying the bigger markets, but consider also the disposable income of the people: China, for example, has the world's largest economy, but 1.4 billion people spreads that wealth

---

2. www.bexa.co.uk/BExA/ExportSupport/BExA-Guides/BEXA/Policy-and-Publications/BExA-Guides.aspx

out dramatically. Per Capita Income is an important measure if the product is a mass market product, but if you are selling luxury goods, the real measure is the disposable income of the richest segment of the population, the A, B, C1 demographic strata.

Checklist: Awareness of local customs and practices

- Check local, national and religious holidays, and summer factory/office shutdowns. The working week may not be 9am–5pm Monday to Friday.
- What is the normal dress code?
- Be sensitive to your customer's religion:

  - Foods or food combinations to avoid
  - Fasting times
  - Prayer times

- Understand the politics and other newsworthy events in the territory, including when elections and major sporting events are being held.
- Understand the business etiquette on greetings and meetings. If in doubt, always shake hands with your right hand, address as Mr/Mrs, and receive a business card with both hands, taking care to read it. Practise these things at home so that you do not feel shy doing them when you arrive.
- Smiles can go a long way, but don't try British or self-deprecating humour too early in your relationship, and certainly not by email where it can be read very differently. Taking the blame and playing the eccentric Brit can have benefits, so long as you don't repeat this too often.

MAKE IT A BUSINESS

Don't try to take on overseas markets until you have the resources (in terms of people and money) to do things properly. Too often people go into exporting via an export agent, assuming this will be a useful add-on for the domestic business, but it isn't wise to treat export as an add-on. Take it very seriously. And think: you need to have a success early on or the team will become disillusioned.

This is where working with third parties can help. Much expertise is available from sales agents and export houses, from freight forwarders for the logistics, and the bank and factoring houses who can help with payment and credit collections. You don't have to do it all yourself to be successful!

Choose your customers wisely. Seasoned exporters make the availability of credit insurance on a customer a part of the decision about whether to bid. The value of the credit insurance is that if the customer does not pay in good time, the credit insurer can help with debt collection and, if that is also unsuccessful, pay a claim.

FINANCE

When you start exporting, you will have an extra cash requirement. Suppliers may demand payment at 30 days, but because the goods take longer to get to their destination, you have to give longer credit on your sales. You may need to compete with local suppliers in your destination market where the usual credit terms may be longer. For example, Germany and Netherlands companies tend to pay strictly 30 days after invoice date; whereas in France and Belgium, 60–90 days is the norm and Portugal, Spain, Greece and Italy ask for long credit terms and take longer to pay! How will you fund this? You may be able to negotiate longer terms from suppliers because you are winning more business for them. Export factoring can be used to close the gap. However, factoring only works once the sale has been made. Prior to that, you may need to look at procurement finance or sources of additional working capital, not forgetting 'non-bank finance' such as peer-to-peer lending. The Government has an Export Working Capital Scheme to help address the working capital needs of exporters.[3] See also BExA's Guide to Financing Exports.[4]

> Terms of payment must relate to something under your control; the despatch date or invoice date are usual. Avoid '30 days from date of arrival at customer's site': What if the goods are delayed? How do you prove they have arrived? What if your goods arrive at the beginning of a public holiday and have to be stored?

ROUTE TO MARKET

Work out how you are going to get the goods there, including delivery (Incoterms®) and management/organisation. Use the four Ps:

Product – what are you selling; how is it packaged, what are the warranty obligations? What substitute product is available? Will you have issues with Intellectual Property?

---

3. Details of Government Export Finance schemes can be found on the UK Export Finance website: www.gov.uk/government/organisations/uk-export-finance
4. Guides available to download at www.bexa.co.uk

Place – destination; how you will transport the goods there, how you will get them in front of your customer. What is your method of distribution/logistics? Who will provide after-sales services?

Price – check what else sells in the market and at what price. What are the usual payment terms, and what will you have to offer to be competitive?

Promotion – how do you get the customer to buy? How do you get the message out – advertising, trade shows, brochures, sales force, distributors? Will you sell directly or engage a local representative? How does the local market normally sell goods?

Sometimes it is better not to follow the crowd. One British exporter had a choice of two trade shows: Moscow supported by DIT or Prague with no support. The exporter writes: 'We went to Prague and were the only foreign company. We established business with four different Czech importers.'

WHERE TO START

Identify your new market from research with the help of DIT. British embassies and consulates, through their commercial staff, provide invaluable help to new exporters in a number of different ways, including helping identify potential agents and local organisations and give you an understanding of local commercial practices. There is no substitute for visiting the market. Consider taking part in a trade mission organised by a UK Chamber of Commerce or Trade Association. And get networking: experienced exporters are usually happy to share their experiences of overseas markets.

2.3

UNDERSTANDING INCOTERMS AND THEIR USAGE

Jonathan Reuvid

INTRODUCTION

For export prices to make any sense there must be some expression as to what is included and not included in any price quoted. The specific definition of the 'trade terms' or 'delivery terms' that apply contractually to each order is necessary. Over centuries of international trading a range of standard expressions to cover most types of sales contracts has evolved.

Perhaps the most important landmark was in 1936 when the International Chamber of Commerce (ICC)[1] published the first version of Incoterms which set out to codify standardised and globally accepted definitions of the seller's and buyer's obligations under a range of terms in current use worldwide. Since then ICC has produced revised terms at intervals to coincide with the first year of each decade from 1990. The new Incoterms published in November 2019 came into force from 1 January 2020 and marked the beginning of ICC's centenary year.

ICC Incoterms® 2020 were drafted by a Committee of Experts, mainly representatives of European Chambers of Commerce and now including representatives from China and Australia. They reflect and

---

1. www.iccwbo.org

discuss the various issues raised by the 150 ICC members from time to time. The newest terms include more detailed explanatory notes than the previous version with improved graphics to illustrate the responsibilities of exporters and importers under each Incoterms® rule. The introduction also includes detailed advice on how to select the most appropriate rule for each transaction and how a sales contract interacts with other relevant contracts.

It is important to recognise that while ICC Incoterms® 2020 regulate the physical transfer of goods and commodities from seller to buyer they are silent on the transfer of title and how goods are to be paid for. Exposure to financial risk is addressed in Chapter 2.5.

CONTEXT AND CATEGORIES OF INCOTERMS

The language agreed by the ICC in their guidance covers the following areas of international trade and commerce:

- Which parties hold contract
- Tasks involved in shipping
- Delivery of goods (sellers and buyers)
- Insurance obligations
- Customs and taxes
- Responsibility of risk

Basically Incoterms® are the terms which apply to any mode of transport and terms which apply only to shipments by sea (or inland waterway); there are changes to the standard terms in the 2020 rules from those where shipments were made under the old ICC Incoterms® 2010. The definitions of terms below are those that now apply for new contracts.

'Any mode' terms

EXW (Ex Works – named place)
Although applicable to any mode of transport, EXW is only appropriate for domestic transactions and now less frequently used for home sales. The seller is only obliged to 'render the buyer... every assistance in obtaining any documents' and has no obligation to load the goods. The buyer has limited obligations to provide the seller with proof of export, rendering this mode unsuitable for today's international trade.

FCA (Free Carrier – named place)

With minimum obligations, this is the preferred Incoterm for international trade from the seller's point of view. It has the advantage, when compared with EXW, that because the seller is responsible for any export licensing and export clearance the problem of proof of export is eased. The seller must also load the goods, but that is normal in practice. FCA is versatile and allows for delivery in a variety of locations (e.g. land transport terminal, port or airport) that are usually in the seller's own country. However, the buyer is responsible for unloading the goods and the risk passes to the buyer when delivery is made. The seller is responsible for export formalities and the buyer for import formalities.

In the ICC Incoterms® 2020 FCA, includes arrangements for carriage with own means of transport, either DAP (Delivered at Place), DPU (Delivered at Place Unloaded) or DDP (Delivered Duty Paid). The old DAT (Delivered at Terminal) is now abandoned and changed to DPU. The old DAT rules assumed third-party carriage.

CPT (Carriage Paid To)

This rule requires the seller to deliver goods to the carrier but does not state whether loading takes place at the seller's premises loaded on to the collecting vehicle or whether delivery is to other premises unloaded from the seller's vehicle. The seller is required to carry out all export formalities and to contract for carriage with the cost built into the selling price. The buyer is responsible for any import formalities. As with FCA the risk passes from seller to buyer when delivery is made.

CIP (Carriage and Insurance Paid To)

The one critical difference from CPT is that under the CIP rule the seller is obliged to take out maximum insurance cover for the buyer's risk under Institute Cargo Clauses (A) or (Air). Any insurance documents that the buyer would need in the event of a claim under the insurance must be passed to the buyer.

DAP (Delivered at Any Place Unloaded – UPDATED)

The seller is required to a place named by the buyer, often the buyer's own premises. The buyer is responsible for unloading the means of transport when delivered. While the seller is obliged to carry out the export formalities, the buyer is responsible for all import customs formalities and costs.

As with CPT and CIP (both for maritime use only), the seller contracts for carriage and the risk transfers to the buyer only upon delivery. The seller is not obliged to take out insurance cover for the buyer's risk. Although DAP works well for deliveries across the Europe/Asia landmass there may be problems with DAP in the event of a change of transport *en route*.

The DAP term replaced the old DAF, DES and DDU terms in 2010. The new terms apply when 'the goods are placed at the disposal of the buyer... ready for unloading by the buyer at the named place.'

DPU (Delivered at Place Unloaded – named place of delivery)
Relates in practice to what happens across the Europe/Asia landmass when goods are delivered by the same transporter across the EU and frontiers further East. It also represents what happens with courier parcels where the driver delivers direct to the consignee's door and can also work for lighter airfreight parcels which the driver can lift unaided.

The Institute of Export and International Trade comments that there are uncertainties how DPU will work out post-Brexit for heavier airfreighted packages and cross-channel container shipments to the EU in respect of paperwork, insurance and workplace safety issues.[2]

DPU replaces DAT (Delivered at Terminal), which in turn replaced DEQ (Delivered Ex Quay) in 2010.

DDP (Delivery Duty Paid – named place of delivery)
There is one critical difference between this rule and DAP which makes it dangerous for the seller's use. Under DDP the seller is required to import clear the goods in the buyer's country and pay any duties and VAT/GST. If there is any doubt that the seller can qualify as the importer or unable to recover any VAT/GST paid, DAP terms should be adopted instead.

'Maritime only' terms
Unchanged from Incoterms® 2010, these rules may still be used for bulk commodities.

---

2. Bachelor, L. (2019), Institute of Export and International Trade, Trade Global Finance, London

FAS (Free Alongside Ship – named port of shipment)
Dating back centuries, the FAS rule requires the seller to physically place the goods alongside the vessel nominated by the buyer and should be applied only for maritime use (or inland waterway) transport. When the goods are containerised, the FCA term should be used.

FOB (Free On Board – at named port of shipment)
The old ICC Incoterms FOB and CIF of longstanding usage, for which FCA and CIP are replacements, are still being used by many exporters and agents involved in international trade (freight forwarders, logistics operators, banks *et al.*) Since some 80% of world trade is transported by container, it is important that the FCA term is used. Like CIF, FOB continues contractually and it is up to the seller and buyer to define what they mean by FOB.

CFR (Cost and Freight – to named port of destination)
Again, a commonly used trade term used without reference to any Incoterms® rules, the parties to a contract using this acronym need to define what they mean. As with FAS, CFR is unsuitable for container shipments.

CIF (Cost Insurance and Freight – to named port of destination)
Differing from CFR in one respect only, the CIF rule requires the seller to take out the minimum level of insurance cover for the buyer's risk, although the risk transfers from the seller when the goods are loaded on board the vessel.

APPLICATION AND COMPOSITION OF INCOTERMS

Exporters need to be clear that Incoterms® 2020 refer to the sales contract and **not** to the transport contract and are not 'laws'. Their legal effect resides in the will of both parties to choose and make explicit written reference to them in their commercial transactions.

Obligations of the parties under ICC Incoterms® 2020
The parties' obligations do not extend to:

- Transfers of property or any other sales right
- Breaches of contract and their consequences
- Financial conditions and liabilities arising from execution of the main legal transaction.

Under each term the rules governing the performance obligations of both seller and buyer are codified and set out responsibilities as follows:

Seller's obligations	*Buyer's obligations*
A1. General obligation	B1. General obligations
A2. Delivery	B2. Taking delivery
A3. Transfer of risks	B3. Transfer of risks
A4. Carriage	B4. Carriage
A5. Insurance	B5. Insurance
A6. Delivery / transport document	B6. Proof of delivery
A7. Export / import clearance	B7. Export / import clearance
A8. Checking / packaging / marking	B8. Checking / packaging / marking
A 9. Allocation of costs	B9. Allocation of costs
A10. Notices	B10. Notices

KEY SHIPMENT DOCUMENTATION

For exporters there is a range of documents that shipping and forwarding agents, contracted transporters and customers or their agents will need in the course of physical delivery of goods to their specified destinations; they are mostly cited in ICC Incoterms® 2020 rules.

Bill of Lading (BL) for Ocean Freight

Referred to in shipping and trading documents, particularly in the case of cross-border transactions or the movement of goods overseas, the Bill of Lading is a list of the cargo to be carried provided by the master of the ship to the consignor as a receipt.

The BL needs to be a negotiable document and can take a variety of forms.[3] Its three purposes are:

- a definitive receipt (goods are loaded)
- document of title to goods
- terms of carriage contract

There are two categories of BL:

- **On board bill of lading** where there is no discrepancy between the goods actually on the vessel;

---

3. See Trade Finance Global at www.tradefinanceglobal.com/freight-forwarding/bill-of-lading

- **A clean bill of lading** showing that goods have been loaded on board. If the carrier finds that the BL differs from goods on board, evidence can be cited on the clean BL. Once the BL has been transferred to a third party it is not possible to mark a discrepancy. A 'claused bill of lading' is when the difference is visible on the BL

A BL is usually classed as a document of title when the purchaser of the goods receives them from the carrier. Classification may be either as a 'straight BL' issued to a specific consignee, when it is non-negotiable, or as a 'to order BL', which can be transferred or negotiated to be in favour of another party.

Traditionally, bills of lading are issued in triplicate, with one copy taken by the vessel skipper, one by the consignee and the third by the finance provider or some other party. The use of digital documentation reduces the need for multiple copies. As discussed in Chapter 2.6 ,the advent of standardised distributed ledger (DLT) or 'blockchain' technology will help to solve many of the administrative problems which UK exporters and importers will face in trading with the EU post-Brexit.

While ocean (sea) freight accounts for up to 90% of international trade traffic, airfreight may be an attractive alternative for many classes of goods and requires different documentation.

Master Airway Bill (MAWB)
As with the bill of lading for ocean freight, shipping goods by air requires its own documentation. Issued by an airline or its authorised agent, the Master Airway Bill (MAWB) shows evidence of the contract of carriage.

Individual consignments of goods can be consolidated into consoles with other shippers. Consolidation is cost-effective in principle through economies of scale, but it can lengthen delivery time while waiting to group shipments or pair up.

Certificate of Origin (CO)
A CO is often requested by overseas buyers for customs clearance, payment management and concessions on import tariffs. It specifies where goods are produced, manufactured, processed or wholly sourced in a particular country. Every Certificate of Origin is governed by Rules of Origin as the criteria by which the national source of a product is determined.

Governments follow a diverse range of practices; the rules are negotiated as an integral part of a Free Trade Agreement (FTA) and differ under each FTA. Undoubtedly, CO certification will be an important part of the UK's negotiations when it leaves the EU.

Basically, there are two types of CO, preferential and non-preferential, which differ as follows:

- **Preferential COs** – subjecting goods to reduced tariffs under a FTA or exemptions when they are exported to countries within a customs union (e.g. the arrangement for goods passing through Northern Ireland to the Republic of Ireland, which may be difficult for products whose quality standards diverge from present alignment.)
- **Non-Preferential COs** – also known as 'ordinary COs', where the country of origin does not qualify for preferential tariff treatment.

The British Chambers of Commerce identifies four specific certificates in current use designed to facilitate the movement of goods:

- **EC Certificates of Origin** – customs clearance requirements to evidence the origin of goods.
- **Arab-British Certificates of Origin** – a customs clearance requirement to evidence the origin of the goods which may be requested by the importing company and may be used for the Arab League States.
- **EUR1 Movement Certificates** – used to support claims for preferential rates of duty (usually zero) in the country of representation. To qualify the goods must originate in th UK or EU. The preference system only applies to countries where trade agreements with the EU exist and.
- **ATR Movement Certificate** – entitles goods which are in 'free circulation' in the EU (either EU-originating or with all duties and taxes paid in importation into the EU) to receive preferential import duty when shipped into Turkey. This applies to all eligible goods except agricultural products, minerals and steel, which require an EUR1.

No doubt different certificates will be required for UK trade after the transitional period when the UK and EU have concluded their post-Brexit trade deal.

There is a wide variation in the paperwork requirements of various countries with preferential arrangements under FTAs with the EU; for example, the EU Korea Free Trade Agreement, where the only acceptable proof of origin to claim preference is an origin declaration made out by the exporter under Article 15. New exporters should take advice from customs authorities in the goods' destination country or from the DIT overseas trade division.[4] There are individual rules of origin and tariff preferences for a number of countries which have preference arrangements with the EU including Egypt, Iceland, Morocco, Norway, South Africa, Switzerland and Turkey.[5]

European Union Certificates of Origin (non-preferential origin) are issued by local Chambers of Commerce having DIT authorisation. UK exporters may also apply online through the British Chambers of Commerce (BCC) website for an e-Cert (an electronic Certificate of Origin). America has its own certificate of origin rules and requirements which will apply in the event of a FTA between the UK and the US.

---

4. Another useful information source is the preferential origin handbook downloadable from the Europa website

5. See HMRC Notice 828

2.4

BUSINESS WITHOUT BARRIERS

Glynis Whiting, Managing Partner, TIAO

What if non-tariff, non-physical trade barriers were removed? British chambers of commerce in overseas markets and the UK have started using technology to facilitate international trade around the world.

Restrictions imposed by governments are not the main barriers to trade. The greatest barrier for SMEs is finding the right people to help them do business in a new market.

There is an ever-growing number of online platforms which seek to use the internet to create business opportunities. Learning from Amazon and other giants, many businesses would like to find an easy and inexpensive way to extend their market and develop business. But in the online world, with scare stories every day of cyber-crime and online hackers, how do you know who you are really dealing with?

Traditional face-to-face networking, the tried and tested way to develop business with people you know, like and trust, is often very inefficient. It can be time-consuming and expensive, especially for small businesses and startups with limited resources.

Chambers of commerce have traditionally provided a strong, trusted environment in which companies can build long-term lasting business relationships. Networking events, personal and business development opportunities are the mainstay of the chamber calendar. However, building your business this way can be a slow process, and chambers themselves can find recruitment and retention of their business members in a competitive environment to be challenging.

As Joost Visser, Managing Director of new technology company TIAO says, 'If you look at chambers from a member's perspective, after three or four years you have done the tour of all the other members. Where do you go then?'

AN ONLINE PLATFORM FOR CHAMBERS OF COMMERCE

TIAO has understood that Chambers of Commerce have a unique trust value with their member. For this reason they have teamed up initially with British chambers in mainland Europe and now with wider global chambers in 27 countries worldwide to put together the best of both worlds – the personal and the digital.

The challenge is how to create a global online platform which combines opportunities for every company to do business with each other in an environment in which the key ingredient is trust. Trust cannot be bought – it must be earned, and as we have seen in recent months, in an increasingly connected online world of social media, it can easily be lost.

CONNECTS.World is a matchmaking platform for businesses anywhere to find opportunities to grow their business in a trusted environment 'at the click of a button'.

TRUST IS THE KEY INGREDIENT

'Trust is forever fragile and attempts at control futile. Managing the message simply won't work in today's complex and interconnected world.' – Robert Philips, Jericho Chambers.

Chambers of commerce know their members, often over many years. They also have unique insights into their local marketplace; how it works in practice, what are the key questions every business new to the area needs to ask – and all the answers.

So the CONNECTS.world platform is personally moderated at local level by chamber staff, who can also call on the expertise of their own members – an unparalleled hub of local professional knowledge and support creating a unique trusted environment for new entrants to market.

TIAO itself is predicated on this premise – TIAO stands for 'Trust is an Outcome' and this element is core to how CONNECTS.World works at every level.

WHAT DOES CONNECTS OFFER?

The platform offers four services which together create a unique trading hub for companies:

1. To develop and enhance their profile, searching out the right opportunities
2. A tailored, automated 'matchmaking' service between company members within the network
3. Facilitated transactions between members that have 'found' each other via the platform
4. A route to market to 100 million companies worldwide via our founding partner Kompass International and Open Corporates.

WHAT DIFFERENTIATES CONNECTS FROM OTHER ONLINE PLATFORMS?

*   Multi-level/multilateral – The reach and breadth of the network across Europe and beyond with companies locally and internationally, whether for export, accessing supply chain webs across the world, for joint ventures, investments in any marketplace – business without barriers.
*   Membership-driven in-depth local knowledge in each local chamber/network, from startups to major corporates – everyone can build a profile and reputation on the platform.
*   Moderated – The unique aspect which ensures that the platform is a safe and trusted space in which to do business. Much of the matchmaking online is automated, but there will also, when needed, be personal follow-up by each chamber/network. This personal contact through known networks is a key element which builds trust for all participants.

HOW DOES IT WORK?

There are five distinctive features:

1. Create a profile and upload opportunities
Each chamber becomes a network on the platform and uploads basic information about its members (company name/description/ sector, etc.). Members are then individually invited to activate their membership of the platform (with acceptance of terms and conditions) and build their profile in the platform. This can include

as much detail as possible about who they are, what they do, their key products and services as well as the key people running the company. They can also upload business opportunities – what they are looking for – to offer or state what their needs are. All key words are searchable by others, which increases the opportunity to make the right match.

2. Intuitive search to find future business opportunity or partner

The CONNECTS.World search engine helps define every search using key words that match what is written in profiles and opportunities and other search criteria. Members can refine their search (location, sector, name, size of company and other keywords). Based on the information in the member profiles and the opportunities they have posted, other members can find them. Once they have identified a possible match, members can make direct contact with them via inline messaging directly to the primary contact of their match.

3. No dead ends – guaranteed search results

With TIAO's strategic relationship with Kompass International, every member has access to the 10 million businesses in 70 countries around the world in the Kompass International Directory. CONNECTS and Kompass work with members to select any or all of these companies, to invite them to join the platform, and participating networks have the opportunity to offer full network membership where relevant. Each member can invite other companies to join the platform and develop further contacts.

4. Improve results by building trust

Trust is a combination of three elements: delivery, transparency and accountability. As TIAO puts this at the heart of the platform, every member can improve their results by building trust through their TIAO score. The TIAO score rewards **delivery** by how active they are on the platform, **transparency** by the completeness level of their profile, and **accountability** by how responsive they are and how many opportunities they upload. The higher the TIAO score, the higher the company ranking in searches.

5. Moderation – integrating digital with personal

The role of the chamber/network moderator is a unique element in building trust in the platform.

Each chamber/network has a dedicated moderator. Although most connections in the platform are automated, the role of the moderator is a key differentiating ingredient to:

- Act as a personal point of contact for all chamber members in the platform – this works in two ways – adding value to the membership offer, plus raising the profile of the chamber with new prospects;
- Assist members in using the platform (creating profiles, doing searches and posting opportunities) and support with match-making and business development opportunities;
- Validate applications for new memberships – maintaining trust in the network and providing opportunities to recruit new members to their own network.

The moderator has real-time access via a personalised dashboard to what is happening on the site, so can make personal contact where necessary as well as monitor activity and report back to the chamber and its members, promoting success stories.

A moderators' community has been created, which meets online to develop ideas and share experience nationally and internationally.

IN SUMMARY

At a time of increasing global uncertainty and potential political impasse, businesses need support to weather the storms and navigate in 'choppy waters'. It is, conversely, also a good time to act and take advantage of global opportunities.

People like to do business with people they know, like and trust. Chambers and local business networks are uniquely positioned to deliver real business opportunities because of the unique combination of:

- **Local knowledge** and experience of business reality in each market or sector place, either in-house or via the breadth of existing/prospective members, who may be local SMEs or larger B2B service providers with international coverage;
- **Strong personal, often long-standing relations** with members which cannot be replicated by governmental or single commercial players – ideally placed to provide personal moderation;
- **Global reach** of the CONNECTS network – multi-lateral/multi-level **network of networks**;

- **Personal moderation** – CONNECTS helps chambers/ networks to interact and exchange **best practice**. The Chamber accreditation process is continuously improving the effectiveness and governance of chambers and the growing 'moderators community' assists with the sharing of ideas and experience;
- **User-led** – The platform is being continuously developed, facilitating more **self-learning** to improve the matchmaking.

WHO IS BEHIND CONNECTS?

Launched as a pilot in 2017, CONNECTS.World is now fully operational with 38 partner networks already online, with additional networks joining every month.

Feedback from companies is already positive. As one of the UK's largest electronics distributors said at the Hertfordshire Chamber launch in June 2017: 'CONNECTS is an opportunity to both procure products throughout Europe and possibly sell as well.'

For Oussama El Karkouri, Managing Director of Mercantilia Agency, 'I am happy to have an opportunity to develop my business beyond Morocco's borders and have easy and quick access to connect with dozens of companies in different countries. I invite all companies to join the CONNECTS community and do business without barriers.'

The TIAO team, which has developed the software as a service for CONNECTS, has in-depth understanding of both technology and, more importantly, how chambers and their members work.

Founder Advisor to TIAO is Marc Decorte, former President and CEO of Shell in Belgium and Luxembourg and now President of the Brussels Chamber (BECI) with considerable experience in chambers of commerce and technology startups. Explaining what attracted him to TIAO, he said: 'I only look at startups that have a disruptive element in their business model. They must create a new opportunity that did not exist before. One of the criteria for success is that TIAO starts from the customer, and that's what I liked. They didn't start with the technology. They knew that business was missing an element and that it was an opportunity for the chambers, and from that they generated the idea.

'TIAO has a very clear understanding of what chambers do, what chambers need, what the opportunities are, and what members are looking for. And they can position themselves as partners, rather than suppliers to chambers. That's essential.'

He believes that the platform offers a unique win-win opportunity, adding, 'Being active in chambers of commerce, I see two key elements:

1. The number one hope that members have on joining a chamber is that they will grow their business.
2. Growing business very quickly equates to going international, for exporting, finding distributors and partners they can trust.

'For chambers, being on a global platform is a unique opportunity that nobody else can offer. It's like virtual networking. It creates the possibility to do commercial business in a digital way. If I were a chamber, this would be the tool I would give my members as a concrete offer as an integral part of the value-add of joining and staying a member.'

ABOUT THE TEAM

TIAO is one of the fastest-growing business development platforms in Europe. The founders and team members bring together a unique set of relevant experiences and expertise: experienced serial entrepreneurs, management and board experience in chambers of commerce and governmental agencies, multinational global sales, marketing and strategy expertise, plus in-house tech entrepreneurs with a solid track record of building platform startups and online services.

TIAO has teamed with British Chambers in the UK, mainland Europe and beyond, along with the Belgian Federation of Chambers, working with national and bi-lateral chambers across the world. The reach is growing and as of February 2020 participating chambers include Thames Valley Chamber Group, Hertfordshire, Edinburgh and Dundee and Angus in the UK, with Chambers of Commerce in Belgium, Italy, France, Netherlands, Portugal, Finland, Luxembourg, Lithuania, Romania, Slovenia and Bulgaria in mainland Europe. Further afield CONNECTS members include Canada, Nigeria, Morocco, and Colombia, and in Central America, Belize, Costa Rica, El Salvador, Guatemala, Honduras, Nicaragua and Panama. The global reach is continuing, with recent new chambers including the Afghan Womens' Chamber of Commerce and Singapore International.

In terms of function, new developments in the pipeline include AI to improve and further automate matchmaking as well as support for inward and outward trade missions.

2.5

EXPORT CREDIT AND BANKING

Jonathan Reuvid

INTRODUCTION

Two critical elements which remain for successful exporting are trade finance and payment terms. They are interdependent. On the one hand, few exporters are unlikely to be able to finance the cost of manufacturing or additional stockholding, shipment and delivery to supply new customers in overseas markets within their normal business cashflow. And even if they can finance first orders it will be essential to service repeat orders promptly in order to build sustainable business. Therefore, they will need to secure additional facilities before embarking on any international trade programme.

On the other hand, terms of payment which meet or improve on the terms offered by competitors will be an important feature of the total offer package in attracting new customers. Instead of discussing first the trade finance alternatives that can be negotiated at an acceptable cost and which suit the exporter best, this long chapter focuses on the alternative credit and payment terms that are likely to satisfy customer demands and lead to growing export orders before addressing the question of how to finance the additional business.

TERMS AND METHOD OF PAYMENT

We noted in Chapter 2.3 that observance of Incoterms and associated documents reduces, if not eliminates, the logistical and physical risks of international trade in all but those territories where political risk is severe. However, the use of Incoterms does not eliminate the risk of non-payment to the supplier, and exporters should take this caveat on board from the outset. Therefore, there may be an uneasy balance between acceptable risk and opportunity in agreeing credit terms and method of payment with export customers.

Credit risk in foreign trade generally was exacerbated by the international financial crisis of 2008 and is not considered to have abated since. This comment does not refer to developing countries only and certainly applies to the UK as it leaves the relative stability of the EU to sail in choppier waters. Figure 2.5.1 lists the broad alternatives in methods of payment in descending order of risk:

Figure 2.5.1 – Alternative methods of payment

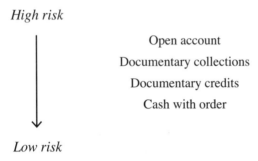

High risk

Open account
Documentary collections
Documentary credits
Cash with order

Low risk

Each of these alternatives imposes different demands on the buyer and seller.

Cash in advance or with order
In certain high-risk countries, subject to their exchange requirements, this is still a normal method of payment and is the most secure for the exporter if it can be secured without damaging competitiveness. In the case of large contracts, a down payment is not unusual with further payment by installments, preferably secured by documentary credits. The money can be transferred as for an open account, with the difference that the transfer takes place before shipment (or even before manufacture) or against a proforma invoice rather than final invoice.

Open account
At the other end of the scale the least secure method of payment, and therefore appropriate for low-risk markets only, is the open account. It is used commonly in Western Europe and the USA, where it is

suitable for established customers but not recommended for new accounts.

The seller will send the goods and all the documents direct to the buyer, using the appropriate Incoterms, and the buyer must then pay on the agreed date. It is important to make completely clear:

When the payment is due
This may be on receipt of goods or documents, which are invariably sent to the buyer, or after a credit period of typically 30, 60 or 90 days after a specified date, usually the date of invoice.

Where the payment is going
The export invoice should specify:

- full company name and business address
- full bank account details
- bank identifier code (BIC, i.e. SWIFT address)
- international bank account number (IBAN)

How the payment will be made
An international bank transfer is the fastest way of receiving payment with importers paying cleared funds direct into exporters' bank accounts, preferably by SWIFT (Society for Worldwide Interbank Financial Telecommunications).

Formerly, before the advent of electronic telecommunications, payments were often made by made by cable or telex transfer (known as TT or telegraphic transfers) or even the slower form of mail transfer.

It is in the seller's interest to minimise the interval between the buyer paying the funds becoming cleared and available. The delay, often referred to as 'float time', is costly for the seller, even when interest rates are at lowest levels, although it is highly profitable to the banks.

Documentary collections
The introduction of bills of exchange, sometimes called drafts, imposes a new documentary requirement upon the seller to draw up the bill of exchange as well as shipping documents. The security offered by the bill of exchange lies in the procedures which involve the banks arranging the collection of payment from the buyer on behalf of the seller.

Having agreed such a method of payment with the buyer, the exporter draws up a bill of exchange which forms a part of the document set that will be sent to their bank. The seller's bank then sends the documents to a bank in the buyer's country, often the buyer's own bank, which will negotiate payment.

The processing of the bill of exchange is illustrated in Figure 2.5.2.

Figure 2.5.2 – Processing the bill of exchange in export trade

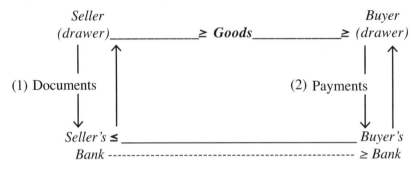

There are various formats for bills of exchange from the traditional versions in Gothic script with ornate borders to the strictly functional illustrated in Figure 2.5.3 acceptable in the age of telecommunications:

Figure 2.5.3 – Typical blank bill of exchange

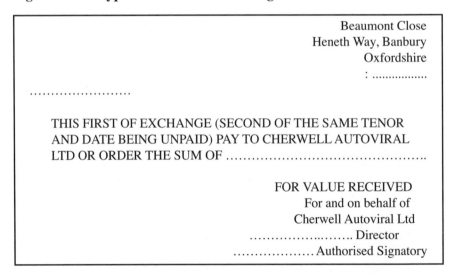

The reason why the bill of exchange includes the words 'first of exchange second unpaid' is that it is common for two or even three bills to be drawn up, based on the rather arcane practice of having two or three bills of lading (see Chapter 2.4) to ensure that at least one arrives safely at its destination into the hands of the buyer or its agent.

Process

Having drawn up the bill(s) of exchange and gathered together the full set of shipping documents, the exporter sends the documentation to its bank, together with a completed letter of instruction. (Major banks have their proprietary instruction forms in tick-box format including clear reference to the procedures to be followed not only by the UK bank but also the overseas bank acting on behalf of the importer.)

The documents will be transmitted either to the seller bank's correspondent bank in the buyer's territory or to the buyer's bank, which will make the collection. A bill of exchange, is defined by the English Bill of Exchange Act 1882 in terms of the information it contains rather than the way it is laid out. By definition, the exporter is the 'drawer' and the importer is the 'drawee'. The drawee is the payer or acceptor of the bill and the money will be paid at the specified time, to the payee, who is usually the exporter but could be another party or even the bearer, i.e. the person holding the bill to claim the funds.

Bills are drawn up at sight or at a number of days after sight, (e.g. 30, 60 or 90 days), or at another determinable future time. Where the amount is payable at sight (i.e. no credit period is allowed) the overseas bank will require the buyer to pay the due amount at sight of the documents. Referred to as documents against payment (DP) the documents will not be released to the buyer before payment is made, providing a measure of security to the seller as the buyer will not be able to take possession of the goods without the documents, particularly if the bill of lading is included in the set.

Where the exporter has agreed to allow a period of credit, then the bill is described as a 'termed' or 'usance' bill. The credit term allowed in the bill may run from the date of shipment (as evidenced by the transport document), the date of the bill or the date of invoice. Either way, the importer enjoys a period of use of the goods before having to pay. In the case of a termed bill the overseas bank will not collect payment in return for the documents but will instead release the document against acceptance of the bill, usually requiring no more than an authorised signature of the payee and a company stamp. The credit term of the bill is known as its 'tenor' and when this expires the bill is said to have 'matured' and will be presented for payment. The procedure is described as 'documents against acceptance' (DA).

It is important to recognise that in cases of DA, there will be no automatic transfer payment when the bill matures. It is still perfectly possible for the buyer to dishonour the bill and fail to make payment. Failure to pay is also possible under DP, but at least the exporter continues to hold possession of the goods and documents. Of course, this is hardly a satisfactory situation since the exporter will either suffer the cost of warehousing the goods at the port of entry (demarrage) and customs duty or return shipment. I recall one case of a manufacturer exporting street-lighting equipment to Nigeria in the 1980s under DA whose customer dishonoured the bill of exchange for more than 6 months, leading to the bankruptcy of the exporter.

Addressing non-payment

In cases of a non-payment of a sight bill (DA), non-acceptance of a termed bill or non-payment of an accepted bill on maturity, it is important in many markets to register a protest immediately – the next day or within the 3-day period of grace allowed thereafter in order to maintain all legal rights against the buyer.[1] Even if the seller has no taste for legal action the filing of a formal protest may prompt the buyer to pay up.

Avalised bills of exchange – an antidote to non-payment

Although a termed bill accepted by the drawee is not a guarantee of payment on maturity, it is possible to arrange in advance for the bill to be avalised by the buyer's bank. This involves the bank adding its 'pour aval' (for value) endorsement or guarantee to the accepted bill. In such cases the seller gains the bank's promise to pay rather than the buyer's. This is not as secure as a letter of credit, because the buyer must accept the bill of exchange first, but it carries the great advantage that the bill can be discounted.[2]

Documentary letters of credit

The ultimate form of bank guarantee used in international trade is the letter of credit (LC). A detailed account of their preparation, presentation and payment procedures is available online from the British Export Association (BeXa) in its guide available online.[3] This chapter provides an overview.

In simple terms, the LC is a letter from a bank promising to pay an amount of money. However, in a typical operation involving the use of letters of credit the promise to pay is conditional upon the exporter providing the documents stated on the LC.

Procedures
The steps followed in sequence are:

- The seller and buyer agree payment by LC with the buyer required to arrange for the LC to be opened by their bank at the time that the order is placed.

---

1. Reuvid, J. and Sherlock, J. (2014) *International Trade*, London, Kogan Page
2. Ibid.
3. Ross, S., (2007) *Guide to Letters of Credit*, London, BeXa

- The exporter needs to review the LC before accepting the order, and checks on acceptability should be made at the very beginning of the order process.
- The buyer instructs their bank, known as the 'opening' or 'issuing' bank to raise the LC having agreed the specific documentary requirements.
- The LC is then passed to the exporter (the 'beneficiary') through the issuing bank's correspondent bank in the exporter's country.
- The bank in the seller's country may simply pass the LC to the exporter, assuming the role of 'advising' bank with the exporter relying on the issuing bank's promise to pay subject to the provisions of the required documents.

  o Sometimes the advising bank (or even a third bank) assumes responsibility to pay by adding its confirmation to the LC and will be referred to as the 'confirming' bank.
  o The exporter may feel that the confirmation of a bank in its own country is more secure than the foreign issuing bank's promise.

- Having received the LC, it is important that the exporter checks immediately to ensure that the documentary requirements and periods allowed are acceptable. If amendments are required, it is advisable to request them at once from the issuing bank through the confirming or advising bank.
- When the LC is acceptable to the exporter, they will proceed with the procurement or manufacture, packing and shipment of the goods so as to generate a set of shipping documents in compliance with the LC.
- These documents will then be presented to the advising or confirming bank in the seller's country who will check compliance with the LC requirements and, assuming no discrepancies, will pay the exporter.

Sadly, reality is not quite so simple. Developed country statistics have shown that in a majority of cases LCs are rejected the first time round due to document discrepancies. A more detailed understanding of the LC process explains why.

Documentary requirements
The norm today is that the exporter will see a hard copy of the SWIFT-transmitted LC perhaps preceded by a an emailed advice; it is based on

a standard format for all LCs involving some 23 fields of information.[4] A typical LC will require:

1. Drafts (bills of exchange), often drawn on the issuing or confirming bank (i.e. the drawee will be a bank rather than the buyer). The bills will state whether the LC is payable on sight or contains a credit term in a clause referring to the relevant LC.
2. Export invoices in a prescribed format and in sufficient numbers. Required certifications and legalisation must be arranged, including certificates or origin or other status documents that may be requested.
3. Insurance policy or certificate, which will be necessary if the contract is one where the exporter is required to arrange for the cargo insurance (i.e. CIF or CIP) to cover for risks and the amount specified. The relevant BeXa guide provides a detailed briefing on export credit insurance.[5]
4. Transport documents, which could be bills of lading, air waybills, road or rail consignment notes or, on occasion, freight forwarder's receipts.

In relation to bills of exchange accompanying LCs, the bank will pay against the sight draft or will accept the termed draft, assuming that there are no discrepancies in the documentation.

Caution These bills are known as 'bank bills' and, if drawn on and accepted by an international bank of standing, would classed as 'good paper' easily discounted by the exporter. However, that is not always the case. As an example, a small Midlands engineering company with whom I was working in the late 1990s engaged in a joint venture in China and, as a part of its responsibilities, trained Chinese machine operators and toolmakers in its UK factory, before despatching the equipment on which they had been working to the JV factory in Jinan.

The transaction was based on a 30 day termed LC which the exporter received direct rather than through its bank. Since the issuing Chinese bank was the same bank that the JV partner, a large state-owned enterprise, used in its general business the UK management did not question that the accompanying bill was good paper and promptly

4. Reuvid, J. and Sherlock, S. (2014) *International Trade*, London, Kogan Page
5. Ross, S. (2007) *Export Credit Insurance*, London, BeXa

shipped the container load of equipment. Only when the bill and LC were shown to its own clearing bank did the UK exporter discover that the paper of the Chinese bank was unacceptable. Fortunately, the Chinese JV partner was able to substitute a recognised confirming bank with minimal delay and payment was made on maturity. An arms' length transaction might have had a less happy outcome.

Additional documentation may be required to accompany the LC including any of the following:

Packing specifications; consular invoices; inspection certificates; clean reports of findings; standards certificates; black-list certificates; phytosanitary certificates; veterinary certificates; halal certificates, etc.

The LC also imposes other conditions on the exporter, most noticeably strict time limits on shipment and document presentations, transhipment and part shipment.

The compliance problems arise when the exporter presents the documents, against the LC, to the advising/confirming bank which examines them closely to assess whether they conform exactly to the LC requirement. The slightest inconsistency, quite often discrepancies in word descriptions which are the result of detailed description, will result in rejection. The justification for the strict level of compliance are:

- If the payment were made by the bank in the seller's country (having not found the discrepancies), it is probable that they would be discovered by the issuing bank, who would refuse to reimburse the issuing bank.
- The confirming bank who pays the exporter without recourse would not be able to recover funds if the issuing bank withholds payment.

However, banks do not reject documents wilfully to their own independent rules but apply the strict set of rules introduced by the International Chamber of Commerce (ICC), known as 'Uniform Customs and Practice for Documentary Credits' (UCP) and followed by 175 countries around the world, accounting for some $1 trillion annually. The current version, UCP 600, was published in July 2007.

Obviously, the exporter should seek to ensure that the LC is perfect before submission; banks and other organisations and other finance institutions which issue LCs provide checklists for this purpose.

It is useful to understand the most common discrepancies that banks find in examining documents presented; the top 10 cited most frequently include:

- late shipment;
- documents not presented in time allowed;
- absence of documents requested in the LC;
- claused bills of lading/carrier receipts;
- no evidence of goods 'shipped onboard';
- description of goods on LC differs from those on invoice;
- documents inconsistent with each other;
- insurance not effective from the date of shipment;
- bill of exchange not drawn up in accordance with LC;
- invoices or C of O not certified as requested.

Consequencies and remedies
The first strategy for an exporter whose LC is rejected is to correct the discrepancies and re-present to the bank. It may well be possible to gain payment by re-presenting promptly. However, the bank could now accept that the documents are correct but reject again because the time limit for presentation of documents has now expired.

If the errors cannot be corrected, the exporter has to accept that they have lost the security of the LC. There are four possibly consequences:

- The bank contacts the buyers via the issuing bank and informs them of the details of the discrepancies. The buyers are entitled to accept or reject the documents as they see fit.
- The documents are dispatched to the issuing bank 'for collection' on the basis that they have reverted to a bill of exchange to collect payment or that they are sent to the buyer's overseas bank for the buyer to inspect 'on trust'. In either case the buyer has the right to reject the documents and therefore the goods.
- For certain discrepancies, such as late ('stale') documents, the paying bank may pay 'with recourse', usually with a form of indemnity from the exporter.
- In the worst case, already discussed above, when the goods are already in transit or have arrived at the port of entry, the buyer rejects the documents and the goods are denied entry clearance.

In summary, the documentary letter of credit is very much a conditional guarantee of payment.[6]

---

6. Reuvid, J. and Sherlock, S. (2014) *International Trade,* London, Kogan Page

Types of letters of credit

Irrevocable
An irrevocable LC cannot be cancelled without the consent of both parties. It can be invalidated only if the issuing bank goes out of business or a government moratorium rules that trading must cease with a particular country.

Revocable
Revocable LCs are unusual and generally undesirable. They may be used between closely related parties where the objective is efficient funds transfer rather than security of payment. Under the terms of UCP600 all LCs will be regarded as irrevocable unless stated otherwise.

Confirmed
As discussed earlier, it may be wise for the exporter to procure the promise of a bank in their own country to pay, by supplementing the issuing bank's promise with its confirmation to the LC. Whether this is insisted upon should depend upon the assessment of the exporter, their bank or source of trade finance of the reliability of the issuing bank.

Transferable
In cases where there is a 'middleman' between the manufacturer and the end user an LC can be raised showing the agent as the beneficiary but also allowing for the transfer of a percentage of the LC to the manufacturer, the difference being the agent's profit. Both manufacturer and agent must meet the conditions of the LC to obtain payment.

Revolving
When a series of identical shipments is to be made it is possible to raise a single LC to cover all transactions rather than a separate LC for each shipment. Such LCs are known as 'revolving' because after payment for a shipment the sum is reinstated for the next shipment.

Deferred payment
Deferred LCs have become increasingly popular as a substitute for raising a bill of exchange under an LC, often because bills attract stamp duty in the issuing country. On presentation of correct documents the bank gives 'a letter of undertaking' to advise when the money will be paid instead of 'accepting' a bill of exchange.

Standby LCs

The standby LC, which neither party expects to be implemented, is used as a precaution in either of two situations:

- Where the seller is trading on open account but requires some form of security, possibly to satisfy the terms of its trade finance arrangements. They are raised by the buyer as a normal LC but require the issuing bank to make payment to the seller only on presentation of documents evidencing non-payment by the buyer on time within the open account agreement.
- To replace performance bonds issued by the buyer under UCP rules as required under most tender procedures.

Summary

The documentary letter of credit is a widely used and very important method of payment in international trade to provide security to the exporter and to their sources of trade finance.

TRADE FINANCE

Focusing on SMEs, small businesses use pre-shipment finance, post-shipment finance and supply chain finance (SCF) and some other facilities. There are varying types of finance and methods of payment for each category, summarised in this chapter. More detailed information is readily available from exporters' own banks or other sources of funds specialising in export finance and the British Exporters Association (BExA[7]).

Pre-shipment finance

Once a business has a confirmed export order from a buyer, preferably backed by a LC, working capital finance is accessible from receivables backed financing, inventory/warehouse financing and pre-payment financing to fund wages, production costs and buying raw materials.

Post-shipment finance

When an exporter has shipped goods, finance can be obtained against payment so that sufficient liquidity is maintained. Post-shipment finance can be arranged in several ways:

- through a LC;
- a loan against an accounts receivable document;

7. Ross, S. (2009) *Guide to Financing Exports,* London, BeXa

- by receivables discounting (selling the invoice or receivables document);
- by factoring of invoices.

Forfaiting

As noted above in the section on bills of exchange, avalised bills (those that a bank has endorsed or guaranteed for payment) may be discounted. There are financial institutions which specialise in such discounting, known as 'forfaiting' at modest rates.

Supply chain finance

Moving into the domain of large companies or smaller businesses that import or export goods as a part of their regular end-to-end supply chains, there is a need for supply chain finance (GSCF) which together with asset-based lending is classified as 'receivables management'.

GSCF provides a cash-flow solution for businesses whose working capital is locked into global supply chains and can benefit both suppliers and buyers. Suppliers receive payment early and can accommodate buyers' extended payment terms. Of course, transactions across borders are subject to enhanced risks and uncertainties and there is an array of risk insurance products.[8]

UK export finance

Finally, there is financial support for exports provided by the government. The operating name of the Export Credits Guarantee Department (ECGD), a ministerial department of the UK government is UK Export Finance; it was established in 1919 and its maximum total global exposure today is reported to stand at £50 billion.

The greater part of ECGD's activities is in underwriting long-term loans for the support of export sales of capital goods. Businesses supported in recent years range from aerospace, construction, oil and gas, petrochemical and automotive to water treatment, industrial processing, healthcare and satellite sectors. However, contracts supported can be as low as £1,000 as well as mega-projects up to and over £1 billion. There are equivalent government-backed agencies in other countries which are major trading nations, such as France, Germany and Italy in Europe or USA, China and India.

---

8. Ross, S. (2007) *Export Credit Insurance*, London, BExA

2.6

PROCUREMENT AND SUPPLY CHAIN DEVELOPMENTS

*Duncan Brock, Chartered Institute of
Procurement & Supply (CIPS)*

*In the context of procurement and supply chain management,
digitalisation redefines models, functions, operations, processes, and
activities using technological advancements to build an efficient digital
business environment businesses gain both operational and financial
benefits, and costs and risks are minimised.*

In this digital era, firms are increasingly investing in technology to
stay ahead of the competition. Though the digitalisation of procurement
and supply chain practices promises to bring barriers down, creating
an interconnected and transparent ecosystem amongst companies,
suppliers and customers, with planned use and implications are yet
to be realised.

CIPS and University of Melbourne carried out global research to gain
insight on the level of understanding of supply chain digitalisation and
what this means for procurement and the wider business community.
This collaboration was primarily aimed at understanding the form of
digitalisation technologies procurement teams have applied or intend
to apply across their company's supply chain practice, the motivations
and benefits behind digitalisation strategies, and challenges facing
managers planning for digitalisation.

This global survey was published in 2019 with results from over 700
managers in more than 20 different industries and 55 different countries

took part in the study. The findings revealed significant developments in how digitalisation is shaping procurement and supply chain management into a transparent, flexible, agile, customer-centric and value-creation system. Companies will no longer operate in physical procurement and supply chain processes; new digitalisation enablers will combine the physical world with the digital. Human interaction will be replaced by autonomous and automatic communications. So it is important to understand the implications of these inevitable changes and how they shape procurement and supply chain management of the future.

DIGITALISATION TECHNOLOGIES AND CAPABILITIES

The research identified eleven digital enablers that companies can use to change conventional supply chain practices and create the building blocks for industry 4.0.

- ***3D Printing***
  3D printing is used to prototype and produce small batches of customised products and individual components, to reduce the uncertainty about the return on investment before a supply chain manager places an order.

- ***Artificial Intelligence (AI)***
  AI machines learn from experience, adapt to novel situations and perform human-like tasks such as visual perception, speech recognition and analysing data.

- ***Augmented Reality***
  Augmented reality is achieved by adding layers of computer-generated information to the real environment.

- ***Big Data***
  Big data is the collection and evaluation of data from different internal and external sources in real time.

- ***Cloud Computing***
  Cloud Computing enables rapid data sharing with minimal effort across multiple sites. This technology can move procurement and supply chain operations away from complex ERP built tools, replacing them with cloud-based analytical platforms.

- *Internet of Things (IoT)*
  IoT is a system of interrelated computing devices, objects and people supported by ubiquitous sensors, offering the ability to transfer data over a network without human intervention.

- *Omni Channel*
  Omni channel is a retailing/marketing tool which connects online shopping, through to bricks and mortar in store transactions, the technology connects the different shopping channels to provide a seamless experience to the user.

- *RFID*
  RFID uses radio waves to read and capture information stored on a tag attached to an object. This touch-free technology can offer increased accuracy and real-time inventory tracking at low cost.

- *Robotics*
  Robots interact with one another and work side by side with humans, by interacting with humans, they learn how to perform both simple, repetitive tasks and more complex work.

- *Sensor Technology*
  Sensors detect events or changes in the environment and send appropriate information to other electronic devices. They can provide important data on the location and the condition of a company's supplies and products as they are transported around the globe.

- *Simulation Tools and Models*
  This technology mirrors the physical world in a virtual model that optimising machine or service system settings before a physical changeover.

Use of digital enablers
97% of the companies we surveyed used at least one of the following eleven digital enablers such as cloud computing, Internet of Things and Big Data in their procurement processes and logistics. These were less complex than the other digital enablers.

Motivations behind digital transformation
Companies interested in digital transformation need to stay ahead of the competition, be agile and flexible and that is why almost 90% of firms surveyed were looking at digital changes to their organisations. Their motivations centred around improving on operational costs and

efficiencies and employee productivity. Making digital investments resulted in reducing costs and complexity in supply chains. The companies surveyed were less interested in brand image, volumes of output or partner relationships.

These companies were keen to develop new business models, as low labour rates and repetitive mass production no longer worked for them.

- Partner relationships – 72%
- Output volumes – 74%
- Flexibility of organisational activities – 80%
- Competitive advantage – 76%
- End to end connectivity – 79%
- Reduction in errors – 83%
- Employee productivity – 84%
- Operational efficiencies – 90%
- Brand image – 71%
- Return on investment – 80%
- Performance of existing systems – 87%

Digital procurement and supply outcomes
Companies with some digital capability reported enjoying more transparency, cost effectiveness, having the customer at the heart of their operations, were more agile and reported improving on effective decision-making. Though these improvements were measurable, they were still in development rather than implemented end-to-end in supply chain operations.

- Effective decision-making – 52%
- Mass customised production – 42%
- End to end integration – 37%
- Customer-centric – 55%
- Real-time capability – 47%
- Interoperable – 46%
- Cost-effective – 57%
- Agile – 52%
- Transparent – 65%

Digital transformation and its challenges
Despite its benefits, companies reported they still faced significant challenges in implementing digital changes in their business.

The challenges included issues such as the costs of technical set-up and longer development time before the systems brought benefits. Both a lack of urgency and a lack of coordination across departments were other obstacles. Companies highlighted that the support of leaders in sharing the digital strategic vision resulted in an appreciation across the business of the importance of digitalisation across the business. The inhibitors to a digital supply chain included:

- Lack of urgency – 37%
- Lack of technological strategic vision – 34%
- Insufficient support from leadership – 34%
- Lack of coordination in the organisation – 38%
- Inability to measure performance – 29%
- Long development times – 42%
- Ongoing support costs – 35%
- Costs of training – 34%
- Technical set-up costs – 46%

Performance post-digital implementation

Only a small percentage of respondents (17–19%) reported better performance compared to their competitors in terms of sales, profit, market share and investment in the early stages of digitalisation in supply chains. Around a third (31–26%) said they were performing on a par with their competitors and the same amount reported their performance to be worse.

- Growth in sales revenue – 17%
- Growth in return on sales – 16%
- Growth in profit – 18%
- Growth in market share – 19%
- Return on investment – 17%
- Growth in ROI – 15%

And finally

In this digital era, customers are more aware of lead times, delivery service levels, and product availability and reliability.

The research showed that companies are determined to implement product, technological and administrative innovations to create added value for both the customers and supply chains through digital opportunities. Digitalisation can create opportunities for improving procurement and supply chain practices to deliver a company's need to innovate and grow.

The fourth industrial revolution is with us now, and companies are re-thinking new ways of how to implement these benefits and what to expect from these digital opportunities. The most affordable and easiest to implement of these digital enablers are cloud computing and the management of big data, though what it means for individual businesses is harder to gauge.

These technologies bring competitive advantages to organisations considering factors such as how easy they are to implement, the low cost of implementation and how to secure ongoing support. However, our research shows that companies should also consider investing in Internet of Things (IoT) that automate the procurement and supply chain processes primarily to save costs. For instance, the automotive industry could save large sums each year with embedded systems using IoT that detects and avoids imminent collisions. IoT integrates with smart sensors throughout the supply chain which can help to reduce operating costs, increase asset efficiency, and improve demand planning whilst also have customers in mind.

End-to-end supply chain integration is also possible, adding sensors such as audio, chemical, electrical, environmental, image, motion and touch or touchless sensors.

It is also inevitable that businesses should invest in technologies such as artificial intelligence and augmented reality, which will become more important in the next few years, before a large-scale move towards these technologies hampers implementation and systems and companies doing the implementation are unavailable. Getting ahead is key. These digital systems create new products, services and business models that bring can bring profits and benefits to many sectors. Artificial intelligence-based platforms can identify hidden patterns in seasonal demands and in the use of historical data. This technology can automate processes such as demand planning and optimising supply chain flows and change procedures to reduce costs, sales cycle times and increase efficiencies.

Augmented reality, which offers a live view of a real-world environment where elements are augmented by computer-generated creations, will be essential in procurement. They can simultaneously generate information around elements such as product costing, contract data, specifications and demand trends to make effective real time decisions.

The use of robotics is more complicated to implement and creates more argument as to its pros and cons. Along with omni channel, and 3D printing which are less popular, and they are more specific to certain sectors and company maturity. For instance, omni channel is a retailing tool which is more popular in fashion industries. 3D printing is mostly used to prototype complex, critical and expensive components before the actual production and purchases are made. Robotics can automate and integrate end-to-end supply chain processes involving forecasting, planning, warehousing, procurement, production, supply and performance measurement which is a potential tool in future.

Robotics are more popular in terms of driverless vehicles, crewless cargo ships and drones.

WHERE TO START

The companies we surveyed found it difficult to adopt digital processes mainly due to the technical set up costs and long development times. However, many did take a small bite out of the digital cherry and build up from that. Alternatives included low cost and easy application choices such as big data and cloud computing as a starting point. But to maintain their hold in the marketplace in this digital transformation culture, firms need certain leadership traits and experiences to make it happen.

Leaders must include digital transformation strategies in their strategic vision reflecting what stakeholders, shareholders and staff can expect with these changes and how to differentiatethe benefits from conventional processes. Rome wasn't built in a day and mistakes can happen. Leaders should provide ongoing support for experimentation and development.

But first they should recognise the level of urgency within the business and the needs of the supply chain before implementation can begin.

In summary, digitalisation potentially produces benefits such as

- Transparency
- Cost effectiveness
- Interoperability
- Customer centricity
- Agility
- Effective decision-making

A toe in the digital water would be a start and companies would eventually at least get the benefits in terms of end to end integration and mass customised production which need more preparation and dedication to achieve a consistent result.

Based on our global survey results, more than 50% of the firms that adopted digital technologies performed better than or at the same level as their major competitors in terms of profit, sales, market share and investments.

From the survey responses, however, it is clear that firms that embrace a digital future can potentially gain economic and operational benefits in the short and long term, providing the will and appetite in the business exists.

Respondents' profiles by industry type
Energy and utilities – 99%
Manufacturing and engineering – 75%
Professional and business services – 50%
Healthcare – 44%
Transport, distribution, and storage – 42%
Government – 33%
Construction – 32%
Fast-moving consumer goods – 31%
Retail and wholesale – 30%
Education – 30%
Banking, finance, insurance – 23%
Pharma and life sciences – 19%
Defence – 18%
IT – 17%
Agriculture, forestry and fishing – 16%
Telecoms – 13%
Marketing, advertising, PR, media and communications – 8%
Hotels and catering – 4%
Property – 3%
Sport – 2%
Arts, entertainment, and recreation – 1%

Responses by region
Africa – 41%
Europe – 35%
Oceania – 12%
Asia – 7%
America – 4%

Annual turnover
Under £10 million – 25%
Between £10 million and £20 million – 13%
Between 320 million and £36 million – 9%
Between £36 million and £100 million – 11%
Between £100 and £500 million – 15%
Over £500 million – 27%

Nature of business
Global – 28%
International – 36%
National – 36%

Number of countries supply chains pass through
1–3 – 37%
4–6 – 19%
7–9 – 8%
10–19 – 13%
Over 20 – 23%

PART THREE

ADDRESSING TARGET MARKETS

patentGate

patentGate – patent information for your company

Patent monitoring with patentGate

patentGate helps you to monitor current intellectual property rights. Based on search profiles, techno-logy trends, and inventions of competitors are retrieved. The patent documents can be distributed and evaluated. Company specific search fields, patent families, citations, and legal status information complete the database.

Reports and data sets: patent profile reports

Patent profile reports contain all recently published documents of the previous month covered by your search profile. Every document includes biblio-graphic data and abstracts with a drawing. We can also provide patent data in other formats such as XML or CSV.

Legal status monitoring with patentGate

We monitor legal status changes of patent documents published in the patent registers of the authori-ties EPO, WIPO, DPMA, USPTO, JPO, SIPO as well as the INPADOC legal status database. You can choose whether you want to be informed about all or only about certain events and receive new results on the fly or as a spreadsheet or PDF document.

www.patentgate.de · patentGate GmbH · Hofgraben 5 · 98704 Ilmenau/Langewiesen · Germany

Coventry University

Enterprise and Innovation –
Supporting Business, Driving Growth

The Enterprise and Innovation team acts as the gateway to business services at Coventry University, being awarded the Queen's Award for Enterprise in 2015. We have a range of ways we engage with businesses from working with entrepreneurs and small organisations to partnerships with multi-national giants of industry.

These include:

- Student internship programmes lasting from a few weeks to longer - depending on requirements
- Opportunities to work with a research graduate to explore new products, new markets and new solutions
- Flexible CPD courses
- Start-up and small business support including free networking events, consultancy and funding advice
- Professional venues and catering for all sizes of meetings and events
- Access to our academic expertise and research
- Office and business incubation space on our award-winning Technology Park

Contact us to find out more about how we could work together:

T: +44 (0)24 7615 8258
E: ei@coventry.ac.uk
www.coventry.ac.uk/business

 **@CovUni_business**   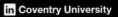 **Coventry University**

THE QUEEN'S AWARDS
FOR ENTERPRISE:
INTERNATIONAL TRADE
2015

BRITISH EXPORTERS ASSOCIATION

BExA

The British Exporters Association (BExA) is an independent national trade association representing the interests of the export community. Our membership is drawn from a wide cross section of companies; Large and SME Exporters, Banks, Credit Insurers and Brokers, Legal firms, Alternative financiers and other service providers – giving us an excellent perspective of the issues that matter to UK exporters.

BExA is a valued contributor to, and is engaged with, many Government departments and committees to drive export policy forward. These include the Department for International Trade and UK Export Finance, the Department for International Development, and attending the All-Party Parliamentary Group for Trade & Industry and Houses of Parliament Select Committees.

Membership is open to all companies and other organisations resident in the United Kingdom who export goods or services, or who provide assistance to such companies in the promotion and furtherance of export activities.

Benefits of membership include:

Representing members
BExA represents members interests on day to day and policy issues relating to UK export and trade policy and on other specific trade related issues raised by members. We meet ministers and Government officials, participate in UK and EU consultations, liaise with other trade associations and obtain press coverage.

The Exporters' Forum
Members meet, exchange views, discuss trade-related problems and update themselves on developments at periodic meetings of BExA's Committee's and sub-Committees. These Committees report to BExA's Council.

BExA Seminars
BExA holds exporter seminars which all members are invited to attend on a complimentary basis.

Networking events
Our Annual Lunch, held in the autumn at the Mansion House, City of London, and our Spring Reception at the House of Commons are prestigious networking events in members' diaries.

Information dissemination
Members receive informative minutes of Council and other meetings, focussed e-mailings on specific topics, and a regular BExA member newsletter.

BExA Guides
The Association has published seven guides 'by exporters for exporters' on key trade issues. The guides are available to download at http://www.bexa.co.uk/BExAGuides.

GTR BExA Young Exporter of the Year Award
This annual award brings recognition to a particularly capable young exporter. For award parameters and to download a nomination form, please visit www.bexa.co.uk/ExportAwards.

Member Discounts and Exclusive Offers
Members have access to a growing list of benefits from the association's service providers. BExA has also arranged discounts and complimentary passses for members to attend many leading trade-related conferences and events.

Member Helpline
BExA offers a dedicated helpline for members that are seeking specialist advice on international trade matters. The advice, which is free of charge to members, covers a wide range of areas including export and import documentation; export control regulations; customs regulations; contractual issues and   transportation & logistics.

Applications for membership can be made online at **http://www.bexa.co.uk/JoinBExA**
For further information please visit **www.bexa.co.uk** or contact:
Michelle Treasure – BExA Secretariat – michelle.treasure@bexa.co.uk – Tel. +44 (020) 7222 5419

PARTNER
INVESTMENT
伙 伴 投 资

TECHNOLOGY TRANSFER
INNOVATION
INTELLECTUAL PROPERTY

equi IP ped[4]

Web: www.equipped4.com
Email: ds@equipped4.com
Tel: +44 (0)151 601 9477
Mobile: +44(0)773 818 5520

Web: www.partnerinvestment.eu
Email: ds@partnerinvestment.eu

Partner Investment
Equipped 4 (IP) Limited
47 Hamilton Square
Birkenhead
Merseyside
CH41 5AR
United Kingdom

TURNING IDEAS
INTO INVENTIONS

CREATE

STREAMLINE

EXPAND

by getting to know your business we become a part of your team; we set, evaluate and adjust the strategy with you

we offer an end to end solution to protect IP rights anywhere in the world using one contact point, saving you time and money

70+ people in 6 countries plus the Aalbun network with over 100 IP experts covering all technology areas and jurisdictions

• Patents • Trade Marks • Designs • Know how • Commercialisation •

basck.com

R&D Tax Credits

How we help Accountants help their companies or their clients.

- Recognising, scoping and describing qualifying R&D work to support claims.
- Auditing previous claims when there is still time to correct.
- Advising companies where HMRC have instigated informal or formal enquiries into claims.
- Situations where companies are using other R&D Consultancies and want to compare service/costs.
- Ensuring companies claim all they are entitled to claim.
- Making sure claims are secure as they can be enquired into by HMRC for up to six years, or longer.

We offer free CPD Workshops for accountancy firms on R&D Tax Credits

Proud supporters of the

fsb MEMBER

frederícksfoundation
now you can.

Helping more than 1250 companies gain in excess of £133m in benefit since September 2012

Tel: 01483 808301
Email: info@randdtax.co.uk
www.RandDTax.co.uk

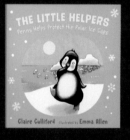

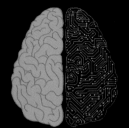
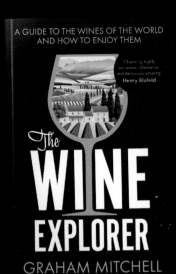
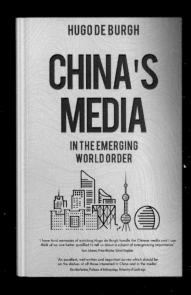
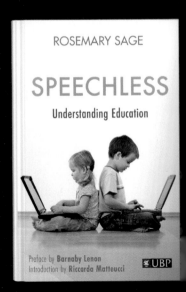

3.1

WTO RULES AND UK TRADE POST-BREXIT

Jonathan Reuvid

RULES AND THEIR OPERATION

History

The World Trade Organisation (WTO) came into effect from 1 January 1995 following signature of the Marrakesh Agreement by 123 nations on 15 April 1994.

The principal features and milestones in its development are:

The WTO replaced the General Agreement on Tariffs and Trade (GATT) which commenced in 1948. GATT followed the establishment after World War II of other new multilateral institutions to enhance international economic cooperation; in particular the International Monetary Fund (IMF) and the World Bank, two further components of the Bretton Woods system.

- Most of the features on which the WTO focuses today have their origins in previous trade negotiations from the Uruguay Round (1986–1994).
- The WTO oversees and arbitrates upon the regulation of trade between members by providing:
    - o a negotiating framework for new trade agreements or amendments;
    - o a dispute resolution process aimed at enforcing members' compliance to WTO agreements.

- The Doha Development Round focused on developing countries was launched in 2001; the original deadline of 1 January 2005 for its work programme of 21 subjects was missed and the round is still incomplete.
- As a result of this stalemate the launch of a further round has been impossible and the number of bilateral free trade agreements between governments has proliferated.[1]
- Under GATT a series of plurilateral agreements on non-tariff barriers aimed at improving the system were drafted, but because they were not accepted by the full GATT membership, they were informally called 'codes'. Several of these codes were amended in the Uruguay Round and adopted as multilateral commitments accepted by all WTO members.
- In the Marrakesh Agreement a list of some 60 agreements, annexes, decisions and understandings were adopted. The agreements fall into six main parts:

  o Agreement establishing the WTO;
  o Multilateral Agreements on Trade in Goods;
  o General Agreement on Trade in Services;
  o Agreement on Trade-Related Aspects of Intellectual Property Rights;
  o Dispute settlement;
  o Reviews of governments' trade policies.

Principles of the trading system

The WTO's role is to establish a framework for trade policies by setting the rules rather than specifying defined outcomes. The five key principles of both the GATT pre-1994 and the WTO are:

Non-discrimination

The two components embedded in the main WTO rules on goods, services and intellectual property are:

- *The most favoured nation (MFN)* rule requiring a member to grant the most favourable conditions under which it allows trade in a certain product type to be applied to trade with all other WTO members, i.e. a special favour granted to one member must be granted to all others.
- *National treatment* requiring that imported goods should be treated no less favourably than domestically produced goods, at least post-market entry.

---

1. Reuvid, J. (2017) *Business Guide to the United Kingdom*, London, Legend Business Books

Exceptions to the MFN principle allow for preferential treatment among members of a regional free trade area or customs union, such as the EU or the North American Free Trade Area (NAFTA), or for developing countries.

Reciprocity

A rule reflecting both the intention to limit free-riding which might arise under the MFN rule, and the intention to obtain better access to foreign markets.

Binding and enforceable commitments

The tariff commitments made by WTO members on accession and in multilateral trade negotiations are scheduled in a list of concessions which establish 'ceiling bindings'.

A country can change its bindings, but only after negotiation with its trading partners. This could involve compensating partners for loss of trade. If a country does not receive satisfaction, the complainant may invoke the WTO dispute settlement procedures.

Transparency

WTO members are required to publish their trade regulations. Periodic country-specific reports through the Trade Policy Reviews Mechanism (TPRM) supplement internal transparency requirements. The WTO also tries to discourage the use of quotas and other measures used to set limits on quantities of imports.

Safety valves

Governments are able to restrict trade in specific circumstances under the WTO Agreements such as measures to protect the environment, public health, animal and plant health. The provisions fall within one or more of the following:

- articles allowing the use of trade measures to achieve non-economic objectives;
- articles safeguarding 'fair competition': environmental protection measures must not be used to disguise protectionist policies;
- articles permitting intervention in trade for economic reasons.

Decision-making and dispute resolution

Self-described as 'a rules-based, member-driven organisation – all decisions are made by the member governments, and the rules are the outcome of negotiations among members', the WTO has adopted the practice of consensus as the dominant process in decision-making.

Nevertheless, the WTO Agreement foresees occasions when consensus cannot be reached and provides a dispute settlement system embodied in the Understanding on Rules and Procedures Governing the Settlement of Disputes (DSU) annexed to the Final Act signed in Marrakesh in 1994.

The DSU is regarded by the WTO as a keystone of the multilateral trading system and cited as a 'unique contribution to the stability of the global economy'.

How the DSU operates

The settlement process involves the appointment of case-specific panels by the WTO's Dispute Settlement Body (DSB), the Appellate Body, the Director-General and the WTO Secretariat together with arbitrators and advisory experts.

The process provides for the process to be carried out in a timely and efficient manner, normally with a panel ruling within one year and no more than 16 months if the case is appealed. Consideration should be even quicker in cases deemed urgent by the complainant.

Crucially, WTO member nations are obliged to accept the process as exclusive and compulsory.

Members

There are 164 WTO members with Liberia (2016) and Afghanistan (2016) being the two most recent. The EU, and each EU country in its own right, are members.

WTO members do not have to be fully independent states; it is sufficient that they have full autonomy in the conduct of their external commercial relations. For example, Hong Kong has been a member since 1995, predating the Republic of China which joined in 2001 after 15 years of negotiations.

As of 2007, WTO member states represented 96% of global trade and almost 97% of global GDP. In 2017, there are also 22 observer governments. Except for the Holy See, they must start accession negotiations within five years of becoming observers.

Accession

The process of becoming a WTO member takes an average of about five years, but it can last longer if the country is not fully committed or if political issues intervene. Essentially, the process for each applicant country is determined by the current trade regime and its stage of economic development. The longest on record was that of Russia, which applied to join GATT in 1993, was approved for WTO membership at the end of 2011 and acceded in August 2012. An offer of accession is only given once consensus is achieved among interested parties.

Accession process

The first step for a country wishing to accede to the WTO is to submit an application to the General Council in a memorandum with a description of its economic policies and all aspects of its trade relevant to WTO agreements. The memorandum is examined by a working party open to all interested WTO members.

The working party concentrates on issues of discrepancy between WTO rules and the applicant's international and domestic trade policies and laws after studying all necessary background information.

In the second phase of its deliberations the working party determines the terms and conditions of entry into the WTO and may consider a transitional period to allow time for the applicant nation to comply with WTO rules.

The third phase of the working party's programme involves bilateral negotiations between its members and the applicant nation regarding commitments and concessions on tariff levels for goods and services. Although the new member's commitments are negotiated bilaterally they are to apply to all WTO members under normal rules of non-discrimination.

In the final phase of the process, on conclusion of the bilateral talks, the working party sends an accession package to the general council or ministerial conference, which includes:

- a summary of all the working party meetings;
- the Protocol of Accession (draft membership treaty);
- schedules of the member-to-be's commitments.

When the terms of accession have been approved by the General Council or the Ministerial Conference, which usually meets every two years, the applicant's parliament must ratify the Protocol of Accession before it can become a member.

Some countries have undergone a rougher and longer accession process than the five years norm because of challenges by other WTO members during the period of negotiations. For example, negotiations with Vietnam took more than 11 years before it was admitted.

On accession member countries must sign all WTO agreements, of which there are currently about 60 having the status of international legal texts.

BREXIT AND BEYOND

Prior to the UK's EU referendum of 23 June 2016, Roberto Azevêdo, WTO Director-General, warned that the UK would face complex talks with the WTO following Brexit. There was a common assumption among many reviewing what would happen when the UK formally left the EU that the UK could simply operate as an ordinary WTO member. In the end this will happen but the circumstances are unprecedented and getting there might not have been straightforward.

The negotiation process

Under the umbrella of EU membership and as a member in its own right, adjustments were of a mainly technical nature. However, the resolution of the WTO membership was needed to accommodate the UK. A degree of careful diplomacy was required and the outcome will be confirmed during the process of the UK's further negotiation of trade terms with the EU following the Withdrawal Agreement.

These negotiations will be necessary to establish the UK's legal status in its own right within the WTO because its present membership terms are integrated into those of the EU. Both the UK and the EU will have to negotiate simultaneously with the rest of the WTO's members to extract their separate membership terms. The negotiation of free trade agreements post-Brexit with the EU itself, the US or any other WTO members on the British Government's priority list of trade partners will be separate, but they will feed into discussions with the WTO. In effect, the original membership access process will have to be repeated in abbreviated form.

However unlikely, just one objection from any trading nation or group of nations which is a WTO member would be sufficient to hold up the talks.

Key issues

The cause of much complexity lies in the EU's unusual situation in the WTO as 29 members: the EU itself and each of its 28 member states. The EU has agreed to keep its import duties within certain limits which apply to all its members when they import from outside the EU. The quotas agreed with the WTO allowing the EU to import maximum quantities of certain products to be imported at preferential lower-duty rates apply to the single market as a whole and not to individual countries. Likewise, limits on agricultural subsidies are also for the entire EU.

Becoming an independent WTO member involves carving the UK's own rights and obligations out of the EU's and that requires agreement with Brussels negotiators.

There is a further complication. Most of the EU's current commitments to the WTO on quotas and subsidies are unknown or obscure for the reason that all the confirmed commitments pre-date 2004, when there were only 15 member states. In the intervening 13 years EU membership has expanded three times, and there has been no agreement with the WTO membership on revised commitments. Shares of agricultural subsidies are likely to be particularly difficult to agree.

Other issues may be simpler, not involving a similar amount of implied work where the UK might assume existing EU commitments and no changes are required. Among these are:

- the EU's ceilings on tariffs;
- market opening pledges in services sectors;
- EU regulations on food safety, animal and plant health;
- product standards and labelling.

The bottom line

However much of the EU's commitment can be simply translated into UK undertakings, with some application of EU rules, there will still be a heavy workload to be undertaken in completing the task. Throughout the process, agreement on detailed issues as well as the complete accession package will be subject to the WTO rule of members' consensus.

The negotiation process since June 2016 to achieve the Withdrawal Agreement was certainly tortuous. There is no reason to believe that the negotiations on trade terms and the UK's status as a continuing WTO member will be any less fraught with difficulties.

LIVING WITH WTO TARIFFS

Trading with the EU

Having concluded the Withdrawal Agreement, the UK will continue to enjoy free trade with the EU during the period of negotiating trade terms until 2021 with provision for up to two years' extension and will maintain the present Common Customs Tariff (CCT) duty rates which the EU applies to imports from countries outside the EU with which there are no bilateral trade agreements.

These rates represent the maximum rates which could be applied to imports from the UK thereafter in the unlikely event of no trade deal with the EU. They vary according to product category from 1 to 45% as illustrated in Table 3.1.1 below. The CCT on pharmaceuticals is held at 0%.

Table 3.1.1 – CCT duty rates on imports by the EU

Selected Product description	Average CCT duty rate (%)
Mineral fuels, oils and products of distillation	1
Nuclear power components	2
Vehicles, parts and accessories	6
Electrical machinery, equipment and parts	3
Plastics and plastic products	6
Chemical products	5
Beverages, spirits and vinegar	4
Items of clothing and accessories (not knitted or crocheted)	11
Knitted or crocheted items of clothing	12
Footwear	11
Meat	5
Dairy products	6
Fish and shellfish	11
Preparations of vegetables, fruit, nuts and other plant products	17
Preparations of meat, fish and shellfish	18
Sugars and sugar confectionery	11
Vegetables, roots and tubers	9
Tobacco	45

Source: https.//www.agendari.com/wto-tariffs-explained/

After concluding its trade deal with the EU, these are the maximum import tariff rates which the UK is likely to adopt in order to be competitive with EU rivals when importing from countries other than those with whom it has signed bilateral Free Trade Agreements (FTAs).

In the event that the UK had left the EU without a Withdrawal Agreement these rates would have applied to exports from the UK to the EU. The product categories in Table 3.1.1 are listed in descending order of the 2015 value of UK exports to the EU. Had CCT been applied then to UK products the total CCT would have been £2.9 billion on exports of £74.3 billion. The top three categories, amounting to £45.3 billion would have accounted for 63% of those exports. Therein lay core concerns for British manufacturers.

Bilateral and plurilateral agreement
During the extended period of negotiating the Withdrawal Agreement, the UK has signed trade agreements which take immediate effect

having left the EU with 24 countries and trading blocs. The most significant in terms of current trading links are:

South Korea
Switzerland (*)
Norway and Iceland (** and *)
South Africa
Southern Africa Customs Union and Mozambique (SACU+M) trade bloc
Eastern and Southern Africa (ESA) trade bloc
Israel
Morocco
* *members of European Free Trade Association (EFTA)*
** *member of the European Economic Area*

Negotiations under discussion on various forms of Agreement from Free Trade Agreement or Customs Union to Economic Partnership with 21 further territories will continue during the period of trade deal negotiation with the EU. Since they are unsigned as the UK leaves the EU, they will now take place under WTO rules.

Only three countries among the 21 (Japan, Canada and Turkey) each accounted for more than 1 per cent of UK foreign trade in 2015 (5% in total).

EU trade agreements and further targets
The EU already has 36 trade agreements signed and in force and a number of others provisionally applied and in negotiation. Of those signed and in force, 14 are on the list of states with whom the UK has also signed agreements.

Following conclusion of a comprehensive trade deal with the EU the UK expects to sign deals with the remaining 12 states with whom the EU is engaged on parallel terms.

Among further UK and EU targets for trade deals, the United States and China predominate. Although the US has made encouraging comments on striking a deal with the UK quickly, British exporters should not expect that negotiations will be a walk in the park.

Data Sources
  www.agendarii.com/wto-tariffs-explained
  www.wikipedia.org/European_Union_free_trade_agreements_
  www.gov.uk/guidance/uk-trade-agreements-with-non-eu-
  countries-in-a-no-deal-brexit

3.2

PRIORITY MARKETS – RESEARCH AND STRATEGY

Jonathan Reuvid

FOCUS FOR UK EXPORTERS

In the absence of a hard Brexit the ultimate tariff terms that will apply to trade between the UK and the EU, as with other countries or customs unions further afield, should not be the determining factor in selecting the priority markets on which any UK exporter focuses its efforts.

Regardless of prior or no previous experience as an exporter, it is timely for any company to step back and research forensically the opportunities in 2020 and onwards to grow profitable business, while waiting for normal trade conditions to resume as the Covid-19 pandemic subsides. Having shortlisted the more attractive markets for export development, each exporter can then apply the practical criteria identified by BExA in Chap. 2.2 to grade and select the most promising.

Desk research
The first step, as always in matters of international trade, is structured desk research. There is an abundance of data available on the internet, but much of it is of peripheral interest only and may be disregarded as not pertinent to the main thrust of a disciplined strategic approach.

The sequential process described below is based on applying the Pareto principle to discover the 'low-hanging fruit' by identifying first:

(a) top target economies with the strongest current levels of imports;

(b) the UK share of each specific market's imports; and

(c) the top UK product groups with the most successful export profiles; and then drilling down to:

(d) the markets within each target territory where each UK product group is imported; and

(e) the shares of the UK's major competitors in those markets. Steps (a), (b) and (c) of this sequential process are detailed in this chapter. Steps (d) and (e) are detailed in the Appendices for individual markets.

Caveat

For individual companies the process can be shortened or supplemented where there is a specific lead or a promising niche market outside the target territory list to which a UK competitor has already exported successfully. Such leads may be mined from Chambers of Commerce or Industry Associations, from consultation with the UK Department of Trade and its website or discussion with recommended export agents or distributors. You can also visit the data from which the 5 step process is sourced to research further into markets outside the top 10 and your own more specific product group, if it is not among those addressed in this book.

A. TARGET ECONOMIES WITH STRONGEST LEVELS OF MERCHANDISE IMPORTS

The first part of the opening step is to identify the leading economies in world trade and the top 20 are listed in Table 3.2.1. Exports as well as imports in 2018 are included to give a more complete picture of each country's international trade activity. For example, both the UK, USA and India import significantly more than they export, while the Russian Federation appears as a top 20 exporter in its role as a supplier of gas.

All WTO statistics are cited in US$, the common currency for comparisons in international trade rather than more recent but parochial UK Department of Trade statistics in £ sterling.

Table 3.2.1 – Leading Importers and Exporters in World Merchandise Trade – 2018

Ranking	Country	Imports $ bn	Share %	Exports $ bn	Share %	Ranking
1	USA	2,614	13.2	1,664	8.5	2
2	China	2,136	10.8	2,467	12.8	1
3	Germany	1,286	6.5	1,562	8.0	3
4	Japan	749	3.8	738	3.8	4
5	UK	674	3.4	482	2.5	10
6	France	673	3.4	582	3.0	7
7	Netherlands	646	3.3	723	5.7	5
8	Hong Kong (China)	628	3.2	569[1]	3.2	8
9	South Korea	535	2.7	406	3.1	6
10	India	511	2.6	326	1.7	19
11	Italy	501	2.5	547	2.8	9
12	Mexico	477	2.4	451	2.3	12
13	Canada	469	2.4	450	2.3	13
14	Belgium	450	2.3	467	2.4	11
15	Spain	388	2.0	345	1.8	17
15a	Russian Federation	-	-	444	2.3	14
16	Singapore[2]	371	1.9	413	2.1	15
17	Taiwan	286	1.4	336	1.7	18
18	Switzerland	279	1.4	311	1.6	20
19	Poland	267	1.3	-	-	-
20	UAE	253	1.3	346	1.8	16
	Total	14,735	78.5	12,726	73.4	

Source: World Trade Statistical Review 2019, Word Trade Organisation

---

1. Includes $473 billion of merchandise re-exports
2. Singapore imports of $371 billion include $204 billion of merchandise re-exported

B. THE UK'S SHARE OF LEADING MARKET IMPORTS

The second factor in the elimination process is to review the current status of UK exports to its primary markets. In Table 3.2.2 the top 10 destinations are listed showing both exports to and imports from the UK's top 10 trading partners. In all cases imports exceed exports, as is the case for overall UK trade with the EU and the total of trade with non-EU economies. This time the data is presented in £ sterling

We can see clearly that almost two thirds of the UK's trade, both exports and exports, is with these top 10 markets. Even more striking is the concentration on the top 6 export markets which account for 51.3% of exports and a similar concentration on the top 6 import markets. Five of the six export markets are also the top 5 import sources. Ireland ranks as the 5th largest export market but is only 10th in the UK's ranking of import sources. Belgium lies 6th in the list of export markets but ranks 5th as a source of imports.

Correlating the rankings of Table 3.2.2 with Table 3.2.1 there are three markets in the top 10 global import markets: Japan, South Korea and India, which are not included in the UK top 10 and one in the UK top 10 export destinations, Ireland, which does not appear in the global top 20 rankings. The inclusion of Ireland in the UK's priority export list can also be justified by its ranking of 5 in UK services exports (£14.2 billion in 2018).

Final selection of target markets for UK merchandise exporters
There are two further factors for consideration:

- markets where the EU has a free trade agreement (FTA) which the UK expects to rollover into a bilateral agreement on leaving the EU.
- countries which have already indicated readiness to agree a trade deal.

Japan and South Korea qualify under the first criterion; Australia and Switzerland under the second. To date India has shown little interest in a FTA with the UK and is now excluded from the final priority market listing. The UK's largest target market, the USA, has confirmed its readiness to enter into negotiations and is being treated by the government as its twin top priority for the UK together with the EU.

Pursuing the logic of this research, we arrive at a list of the top 14 markets to which UK exporters should direct their attention:

Table 3.2.2 – Top 10 UK Export and Import Markets for Goods only – 2018, Seasonally Adjusted

Rank	Export market	£ billion	% of total	Rank	Import market	£ billion	% of total
1	United States	51.9	15.0	1	Germany	67.2	13.8
2	Germany	35.6	10.3	2	China	43.0	8.8
3	Netherlands	26.5	7.7	2	Netherlands	41.9	8.6
4	France	24.1	7.0	4	United States	41.1	8.4
5	Ireland	20.9	6.1	5	France	28.7	5.9
6	China	18.0	5.2	6	Belgium	26.4	5.4
7	Belgium	14.0	4.1	7	Norway	20.4	4.2
8	Italy	10.5	3.0	8	Italy	19.0	3.9
9	Spain	10.3	3.0	9	Spain	16.5	3.4
10	Hong Kong	7.8	2.2	10	Ireland	13.6	2.8
	Top 10 total	219.6	63.6%			317.8	65.2%
	UK World Trade	344.8	100.0%		World	487.2	100.0%
	EU	170.7	49.5%		EU	265.0	54.4%
	Non-EU	174.1	50.5%		Non-EU	222.2	45.6%

Source: ONS UK Trade, September 2019

Table 3.2.3 – Top 14 Target Markets for UK Exporters

	UK exports 2017 US $billion[3]	% share of country's total imports
USA	45.2	2.1
Germany	38.6	3.6
Netherlands	24.9	5.1
France	24.8	4.2
China	21.9	1.4
Ireland	20.8	25.0
Belgium & Luxembourg	19.5	4.8
Switzerland	19.3	7.1
Italy	12.6	2.9
Spain	12.8	3.9
Japan	7.1	1.1
South Korea	6.6	1.4
Hong Kong	8.3	1.4
Australia	4.9	2.5

Source: MIT Observatory of Economic Complexity (OEC)

C. LEADING UK PRODUCTS WITH STRONG EXPORT PROFILES

Turning now to the products which the UK exports most successfully, but excluding petroleum, gas, minerals, metals and any trade with Russia (significant only in the category of planes and helicopters or spacecraft), Table 3.2.4 below identifies the top 12 product categories and the UK's current top 6 markets for each:

In five of the 12 categories the USA ranked as the UK's leading market, and was among the first four in three more. Germany ranked first in 3 categories and among the first 4 markets in 6 more. Other EU markets, notably France, Netherland, Ireland and Benelux feature strongly in the top 6 for most categories. Both China and Japan each feature in the top 6 markets for only 3 product categories. Australia does not feature as a top 6 destination for any product category.

---

3. 2017 export totals are shown in US$, the primary currency of international trade rather than £ sterling. The data is drawn from the Directory of Economic Complexity at https//:atlas.media.mit.edu/en/profile/country

Table 3.2.4 – Leading UK Export Products

Product	Export value $ billion	Share of UK exports (%)	Major markets Share of product exported (%)	All %
Motor cars	45.0	11.0	USA(20), PRC(13), D(9.3), BL(8.1), Fr(4.7), It(4.5)	59.6
Packaged medicaments	18.4	4.7	USA(18), D(13), Ja(6.5), NL(6.3), PRC(6.3), Fr(3.7)	53.8
Gas turbines	14.6	3.7	UAE(21), Fr(12), HK(11), Q(6.8), USA(5.2), Ja(3.6)	59.6
Hard liquor	7.8	2.9	USA(11), D(9.8), Fr(6.3), NL(6.3), PRC(5.6), Ir(5.3)	44.7
Aircraft parts	9.8	2.5	D(24), Fr(20), USA(16), Ca(7.2), Sp(3.2), It(2.8)	73.2
Vehicle parts	5.9	1.5	D(21), Fr(10), Sp(6.6), USA(5.9), Sw(5.9), BL(4.4), No(5.4), Ba(3.9)	63.1
Planes/helicoptors/ spacecraft	4.0	1.0	Om(36), Sau(15), Q(7.7), USA(3.5)	71.5
Combustion engines	3.7	1.0	Tu(26), PRC(6.3), D(13), USA(12), Sp(8), Ja(4.1)	69.4
Medical instruments	2.3	0.9	USA(16), BL(16), D(15), Ir(6.2), Fr(5.8), NL(5.4)	64.4
Office machine parts	3.2	0.8	D(14), Cz(11), NL(9.3), USA(6.7), Ir(5.8), BL(5.0)	51.8
Valves	2.9	0.7	USA(16), D(6.6), No(5.7), UAE(3.8), Fr(3.3), Sp(3.0)	37.4
Computers	2.5	0.6	Ir(15), USA(9.2), D(8.1), NL(7.1), BL(6.9), Fr(3.2)	49.5

Country key: America(USA), Bahrein(BA), Benelux(BL), Canada(CA), China(PRC), Czech Rep.(Cz) France(Fr), Germany(D), Hong Kong(HK), Rep. of Ireland(Ir), Italy(It), Japan(Ja); Netherlands(NL), Norway(No), Oman(Om), Qatar(Q), Saudi Arabia(Sau), Sweden(Sw), Switzerland(He), Turkey(Tu), United Arab Emirates(UAE)

Source: Observatory of Economic Complexity

Collectively, the 12 product categories account for 30.4% of UK exports and confirm the concentration on markets to which the UK exports, but Table 3.2.4 says little about its competitiveness against rival exporting countries.

Services

Before exploring in any depth how competitive UK products are in priority markets, it is important to give an account of how important services exports are to the economy and to overall international trade. Table 3.2.5 summarises:

Table 3.2.5 – Top 5 service group exports in 2018, seasonally adjusted

Rank	Type of service	£ billion	services exports% of total
1	Financial services	62.5	21.0
2	Travel services	36.4	12.2
3	Transport services	29.5	9.9
4	Telecommunications, computer and information	22.2	7.5
5	Other business services	95.6	32.1
	Subtotal	246.2	82.7
	Total	297.4	100.0

Source: ONS: Balance of Payments: Quarter 2 (Apr to Jun) 2019

Caveat

It is more difficult to drill down on trade data for services than for goods to quantify exports or imports of service sub-groups. However, those engaged in many services (e.g. banking, insurance, accountancy and the law) will probably have some exposure already to foreign competitors and are better placed than manufacturers assess export market opportunities.

In 2018 the UK's total export of services was £297.4 billion, exceeding imports at £192.8 billion by a comfortable £104.6 billion. The surplus in services offset the UK's deficit in goods of £142.4 billion, leaving a net trade deficit of £47.8 billion. In post-Brexit Britain the overall challenge for UK business will be to increase exports sufficiently to erase the net deficit. The top 10 current export markets for UK services are all included in the top 14 priority markets for goods targeted in this chapter.

THE COMPETITIVENESS OF UK EXPORTERS

There is an Appendix for eight of the UK's overall top 14 target markets, the top 3 EU markets by value, the US, and the 4 priority Asian markets, constructed to show statistically[4] how successfully UK exporters have penetrated each by comparison with their main competitors. The equivalent information may be extracted by readers for other product groups from the same OEC source.

The findings are challenging and suggest that major efforts will be necessary for the UK to improve performance against its main competitors.

EXAMPLES – GERMANY (2017)

1. *Imports of Medical Instruments. Value $9.08 bn – sourced from:*
   USA   24%   Switzerland   7.1%   Netherlands   6.9%
   China 5.9%   **UK**   **3.9%**

2. *Imports of Gas Turbines. Value $9.28 bn – sourced from:*
   USA   39%   France   15%   **UK**   **6.7%**
   India 5.4%   Canada   4%

EXAMPLES – CHINA (2017)

1. *Imports of Packaged Medicaments: Value $14.2 bn – sourced from:*
   Germany   16%   Switzerland   13%   **UK**   **8.1%**
   France   7.2%

2. *Imports of Broadcasting Equipment: Value $9.53 bn – sourced from:*
   Germany   2.5%   Benelux   1.5%   USA   1.3%
   France   0.34%   **UK**   **0.16%**

Of course, the statistical data is only the starting point for analysing market opportunities and developing entry strategies. However, it is clear from study of the Appendices that the UK's toughest competitors in most markets are also its key customers, specifically Germany, other leading EU members and the USA. They have established footprints in priority Asian markets where the UK has no better than toeholds. In overall terms, from a world ranking of 4 in 2015 the UK has fallen to 6, having been overtaken by Japan and France. UK export performance

---

4. The data for all Appendices is mined from the search tools offered online by MIT's Observation of Economic Complexity (OEC).

has languished since the EU membership referendum in 2016,[5] partly as a result of uncertainties about future trading relationships and medium-term concerns about the UK as a supplier, but there are other factors at play.

Business environments

EU membership of more than 40 years has given the UK a working knowledge of the business environment of fellow and EFTA members and the Department of Trade has resources through the commercial counsellors in UK embassies to identify and advise on channels to market. Further assistance is available through BExA and specific trade associations.

However, for the priority markets beyond the EU business environments differ widely and the Appendices for the USA, China, Japan and South Korea include notes about local features of business conditions which in turn demand additional research.

Key factors in market penetration

Experienced exporters will know that there is a range of factors which will determine whether or not they can sell their products or processes successfully in international markets. Most, if not all, are within the reach of the exporter:

- *Product design:* Redesign of the product itself or its packaging to environmental standards may be required to match or outclass competition and IP protection is essential (see Chapter 2.1).
- *Quality:* So long as UK and EU quality standards are aligned there should be no issues in qualifying for EU acceptance. Beyond the EU different standards may apply but are unlikely to be more stringent. There are known differences in US standards which will have to be accommodated in any trade deal with America.
- *Pricing:* For differentiated technical products pricing may not be a determining factor but discounts, credit terms and warranties may influence buying decisions.
- *Availability:* Long lead times are a deterrent. For sales to EU members the UK exporters will have to adjust to living with customs regimes, assuming that the UK exits the customs union, involving faster order turnarounds, increased stockholding and smarter delivery routing. Preparations for a no-deal Brexit during

---

5. The MIT Observatory of Economic Complexity (OEC) notes that the value of UK exports has declined from 2012 to 2017 at an annualised rate of -3 per cent.

2019 may help some exporters in making adjustments. For manufacturers relying on 'just in time' delivery of components, passporting arrangements within the EU-UK trade deal will be critical. The advent of distributed ledger technology (DLT) better known as 'blockchain' promises to be a game-changer (see Chapter 2.6).

- *Payment terms:* Seldom the determining factor, but there is a balance for the supplier between making its offer acceptable and financial risk (see Chapter 2.5).
- *Marketing and communication:* Exporters need to make effective use of IT and social media to attract and retain potential customer attention and generate confidence in the company and its products. Clunky websites, inadequate product information and slow email response are obvious turn-offs.
- *Representation:* Direct sales, the appointment of sales agents or distributors for new exporters are discussed in Chapter 2.2. Effective sales channels are a question of 'horses for courses' and differ widely according to territory. In Germany, for example, the role of technical rejpresentative is widely respected and *Mittelstand* SMEs who cannot afford a national sales force use such agents, representing more than one non-competing company successfully.
- *Customer service:* Gaining the first order is always an achievement, but building up and maintaining a continuing flow of orders from each new customer is the prize and demands reliable customer service. Without a high standard of customer service, export initiatives may be wasted. Here again blockchain technology may have a part to play.

In most of these areas, exporters will look for an edge over established competition. Innovation may provide that vital ingredient. Hence the theme of this book – **innovate globally**.

3.3

OPPORTUNITIES FOR EXPLOITING TECHNOLOGY IN CHINA

Dominic Schiller, Equipped 4 (IP) Ltd

THE OPPORTUNITY

The 21st century has seen China become a leading industrial force in technologies such as artificial intelligence, batteries and telecommunications. However, it is the biopharmaceutical sector where we are currently experiencing massive change.

The biopharmaceutical sector was valued at $237 billion in 2018 and is predicted to grow to $389 billion by 2024. It is a sector where the United States has dominated based on four essential policy components, namely:

- A strong Research and Development (R&D) infrastructure;
- Effective Intellectual Property (IP) protection;
- Integration of global standards of trade, IP and Regulation; and
- Functioning markets with good reimbursement.

The biopharmaceutical market is itself less than a quarter of the world pharmaceutical market, which is valued at about $1.2 trillion.

A CHANGING ENVIRONMENT

In 2006 the Chinese government introduced its report 'The Guidelines for the Implementation of the National Medium and Long-Term

Program for Science and Technology Development (2006–2020)'. This called upon China to master 'core technologies' including 'major new drugs'.

At around the same time China's 11th Five-Year Plan (2005–2010) identified, amongst 16 focus areas, the following:

- Breeding new varieties of genetically modified organisms;
- Pharmaceutical innovation and development; and
- Treatment of AIDS, hepatitis and other major diseases.

This was followed by the 12th Five-Year Plan (2010–2015), which identified biotechnology as one of the seven priority strategic emerging industries, and the most recent 13th Five-Year Plan (2015–2020) which set a target of biotech industry output to exceed 4% of GDP by 2020.

Alongside these five-year plans, China's Made in China 2025 policy includes the following targets for 2025:

- Achieve drug quality standards in line with international standards;
- Develop chemical drugs, traditional Chinese medicines, and biotech drugs focused on 10 major diseases;
- Industrialise 20–30 new drugs;
- Have 5–10 Chinese initiated drugs receive FDA approval; and
- Construct, improve and support the National Drug Innovation System and promote China's Drug Internationalisation Development Strategy.

This coupled to changes at the China Federal Drug Agency (CFDA) and changes in patent law are having a massive influence on technology transfer opportunities in the pharmaceutical sector. Significant changes in regulation and intellectual property are set out below.

Regulatory

- The China Federal Drug Agency (CFDA) became the National Medical Products Administration (NMPA) and joined the International Council for Harmonisation of Technical Requirements for Pharmaceuticals for Human Use (2017), resulting in a project that brings together the world's leading regulatory authorities to achieve greater regulatory co-operation; and
- The introduction of a national rare disease list.

A consequence of the former is that in the first nine months of 2018, the NMPA approved 37 new drugs (this compares to only 6 drug approvals in 2016), mostly drugs produced by foreign manufacturers. In the same period the US FDA approved 41 drugs.

Intellectual Property

- An improved legal infrastructure is enabling foreign companies to uphold their IP in specialist courts (although damages are not yet at appropriate levels);
- Draft amendments to China's Patent Law, published in January 2019, aims to introduce an extended patent term of up to five years based on a marketing authorisation in China (equivalent to a Supplementary Protection Certificate (SPC) in Europe);
- There are also plans to introduce an equivalent to the 'Patent Linkage' regime of the US that notifies patentees of impending drug registration applications via 'orange book listings'. Patentees could then challenge third-party proposed generic applications should their patent rights be infringed. The drug evaluation authority would have the power to suspend these applications by up to 24 months, until a settlement or valid judgment had been reached; and
- A proposed draft, in April 2018, by the China National Drug Administration (CNDA) on Implementing Measures for Pharmaceutical Trial Data Protection. This would see a 12-year data exclusivity term for new therapeutic biologics, 10 years for paediatric drugs and 7 years for orphan drugs.

The combined effect is to provide enhanced IP protection and support enforcement.

Financial

Of course, the development and launch of biopharmaceuticals is hugely expensive, and it is perhaps no surprise that we have also witnessed changes at several levels facilitating finance from China, whether inside or outside of China. Areas of finance which facilitate support of technologies include:

- Foreign Direct Investment;
- Subsidies;
- Investment Funds;
- Venture Capital;

- Taxation; and
- Talent Programs.

The biotech sector is just one example that has benefited from the influence and desire of China to invest in technologies. In the first quarter of 2018, Chinese funds pumped $1.4 billion into US biotech, accounting for 40% of the overall funding.

Looking more broadly at the life science sector, 2018 saw the greatest investment in local Chinese medical start-ups with over one hundred companies receiving over $4 billion in investment.

Some of this investment has been precipitated by changes in practice on stock exchanges. For example, Hong Kong's stock exchange rule changes allowing listings by pre-revenue biotech companies which no doubt contributed to Hong Kong having six out of the top 10 biotech IPOs worldwide in 2018, including the top two (both Chinese companies), Shanghai med tech company WuXi AppTec, who raised US$1 billion, and cancer drug developer BeiGene, who raised US$902 million.

So, with China actively looking to invest in technologies, as exemplified by the biopharmaceutical sector, how should companies be strategically thinking when it comes to their intellectual property and how do they look to access this growing market?

IP BASICS AND ENFORCEMENT OF RIGHTS

China is party to most international conventions on Intellectual Property, but those looking to commercialise their Intellectual Property Rights in China should consider the following:

Patents In China, don't rely solely on an invention patent. Consider filing utility models (a 'mini' patent, requiring a lower level of inventiveness and providing a shorter term of protection) alongside invention patents. Also, consider using divisional applications to protect inventions in different ways. Additionally, ensure you register separately in Hong Kong, considering whether to use your China or European (UK) applications as the basis.

Trademarks China operates a 'first to file' system, and thus it is essential to file key trademarks in China ahead of discussing/ showing products in China. Consider multiple applications to cover:

- The English name;
- The Chinese 'pinyin' name (phonetic equivalent); and/ or
- The Chinese 'translation' (where the mark has a clear meaning).

Since a trademark is a sign that allows a consumer to distinguish the goods or services of one undertaking from those of another, trademark owners should consider all aspects, not just words. Aspects, such as: stylisation, shape and colour may be more easily recognised by the Chinese consumer.

Trademark owners should also undertake clearance searches to determine that their chosen trademark is registerable and free to use before committing to it in China. Also, it is a sensible idea to check that the mark is 'appropriate' for the Chinese market. For example, the number 4 is considered unlucky in China, as its phonetic translates as 'death'. In contrast, the number 8 is considered lucky, as its phonetic translates as 'prosper'.

Whilst China is party to the Madrid Protocol, and can be designated in an international trademark registration, it can be quicker, and more efficient, to file a national trademark in China due to differences in classification (trademarks are registered by class).

As for patents, consider filing your trademarks separately in Hong Kong, since many goods pass through Hong Kong on their way to and from China, thus providing additional, or alternative, enforcement opportunities.

Copyright China is a signatory to the Berne Convention, so copyright arises automatically without requiring registration. However, in China it is strongly recommended that key works are registered with the Copyright Protection Center of China (CPCC), and indeed, if you walk into the reception area of many Chinese company offices you will frequently see copyright certificates on prominent display.

Trade Secrets Businesses looking to commercialise their Intellectual Property Rights in China should ensure that Confidential Disclosure Agreements (CDAs) are used in dealings with third parties. Additionally, you should check that documents are marked appropriately as 'Confidential'. I'd also recommend that they are provided as dual-language documents and that you carefully consider the enforcing jurisdiction.

This leads us nicely to the issue of enforcement of rights, which historically has been a major problem for companies in China.

Enforcement
There are four formal routes of enforcement in China which are briefly discussed below:

Administrative Enforcement This route is through various government agencies that have the jurisdiction to enforce IP rights, and can often provide a quick and low-cost solution. Enforcement is via the State

Administration of Industry and Commerce (SAIC) and its local Administration of Industry and Commerce (AIC). Actions include:

- Raids, and the seizing and destruction of infringing items;
- Imposing injunctions; and
- Imposing fines for trademark and copyright (but not patent) infringement.

At present, this route of enforcement is most suited to trademark matters.

The Customs Route This is primarily used to address counterfeiting, and provides a mechanism allowing an IP owner to record their IP rights with Customs (both imports and exports) on a national database. The owner submits their business details (company registration details and a translation), copies of the IP rights, a 'white list' of authorised exporters, a fee and a power of attorney. For enforcement to be effective, the owner will additionally provide training to Customs officers at key ports and details of known or suspected infringers.

Civil Litigation This is through China's various courts, and is becoming more common, possibly a result of the inception of specialist IP courts in key cities such as Beijing, Shanghai and Guangzhou. Whilst it is incumbent on the litigating company to do most of the groundwork, the court system is procedurally simple and relatively quick.

Criminal Prosecution This is usually initiated directly through the Public Security Bureau (PSB), but a case may be transferred from an administrative agency (where damages exceed given thresholds) and is the most powerful of the enforcement routes, since the PSB has the power to detain suspects, interrogate them and make searches. However, the procedure is generally slow, and thus the former procedures are generally utilised.

Real change or window dressing?

The changes in enforcement, together with enforcers being awarded more realistic damages (see e.g. *Watchdata vs. Hengbao* and *Huawei vs. Samsung Electronics*) demonstrates that real change is resulting from the dictates of China's leadership.

Indeed, President Xi Jinping's keynote address of 10 April 2018, at the Boao Forum for Asia, emphasised that the changes must benefit foreign companies when he stated:

'...We will strengthen protection of intellectual property rights (IPR)... We encourage normal technological exchanges and cooperation between Chinese and foreign enterprises and protect the lawful IPR owned by foreign enterprises in China.'

This statement goes a long way to explaining why, I believe, that the risks are continually reducing.

At the end of 2016, more patents were filed in China than in the United States, Europe, Japan and South Korea combined. In the first half of 2018, a total of 751,000 national patent applications were handled in China, and Chinese applicants submitted 23,000 international applications via the Patent Cooperation Treaty through the State Intellectual Property Office (SIPO), a sign of increasing exploitation beyond China.

Further, a consequence of the new specialist court is that patent enforcement has strengthened with 19,900 patents litigated in the first half of 2018 (up 23% on 2017).

ACCESSING CHINA THROUGH STRATEGIC ALLIANCES

When it comes to commercialisation of technology, there is no one 'best way'.

The three most established routes are:

- Transfer the technology or intellectual property direct to a Chinese entity;
- Form a joint venture with one or more Chinese entities. It is not uncommon to work with e.g. local government and a venture capital (VC) partner alongside a Chinese company; and
- Create a wholly foreign-owned subsidiary (WFOS).

The former effectively amounts to a 'sale', the latter to the technology (IP) owner entering the market directly, maintaining full control of their technology (IP), whilst the middle option sees a marriage between a number of parties bring different expertise to the Joint Venture. This route is likely to prove the most beneficial but can be challenging and has risks that need to be managed. A particular challenge is the management of foreground IP created in China, and a clear policy defining respective Background IP (that the Parties bring to the JV) and the management, ownership and transfer of the Foreground IP (that is developed under the JV) is required.

It is also important to note that technology transfer to China is subject to a regulatory framework, based on whether a technology falls into one of three categories:

- Prohibited;
- Restricted; or
- Encouraged.

If a technology is a restricted technology, an import licence must be obtained before the technology agreement is legally valid. Without this, royalty payments and technical fees (effective ways of transferring monies from China) can't be remitted.

For encouraged technologies policy benefits should not be underestimated and can include subsidies, tax incentives and government support.

The risk that a technology, once transferred, may be stolen, is, to some extent, mitigated by having a strong initial IP position and effective agreements addressing the Foreground IP. The management of this Foreground IP, as stated above, may prove challenging, and care needs to be taken to ensure it complies with the Chinese Technology Import and Export Regulations, of which Article 27 states '*improvements to the technology shall vest with the improving party*'. One approach is to ensure that agreements specify that the parent company has at least a transferable non-exclusive right to any improvement developed in China, and an exclusive right outside of China.

Irrespective, choosing partners carefully, undertaking an effective due diligence process, and investing in the relationship, both before and after forming a joint venture, is essential to a happy marriage. Thus, invest heavily in finding the right partner but don't stop there.

APPENDIX

The Appendix tables that follow for the selected 8 priority markets provide forensically analysed data for top 20 export destination and import origins for each economy in Table I and for UK exports of top merchandise product groups with identification of the top 6 competing countries in each category of not less than $50 million.

All of the basic statistics are culled from Observation of Economic Complexity (OEC) information available freely at media.mit.edu. This detailed data is organised and published online by the Massachusetts Institute of Technology and updated annually. At time of publication the statistics are for 2017 trade.

For readers wishing to explore trade statistics for other markets or product groups, the OEC offers more comprehensive global market information than from other sources. Other sources may have more up to date headline statistics but nothing comparable in the same depth. Agricultural produce, fishing and food products are not included.

GERMANY

Appendix I.1 – Top Import sources and export markets – 2017

Rank	Export market	$ billion	% of total	Rank	Import source	$ billion	% of total
1	US	112.0	8.4	1	China	109.0	10.0
2	France	104.0	7.8	2	Netherlands	89.9	8.3
3	China	95.0	7.1	3	France	69.1	6.4
4	UK	90.3	6.8	4	US	61.6	5.7
5	Netherlands	84.5	6.3	5	Italy	58.5	5.4
6	Austria	62.5	4.7	6	Poland	54.5	5.0
7	Belgium-Lux.	58.9	4.4	7	Czech Rep.	51.7	4.9
8	Poland	55.2	4.1	8	Belgium-Lux.	49.7	4.6
9	Switzerland	54.6	4.1	9	Switzerland	48.1	4.5
10	Spain	43.5	3.3	10	Austria	42.5	3.9
11	Czech Republic	42.2	3.2	11	UK	38.6	3.6
12	Sweden	27.3	2.1	12	Spain	33.9	3.1
13	Russia	27.2	2.0	13	Hungary	29.2	2.7
14	Hungary	26.1	2.0	14	Japan	24.5	2.3
15	Japan	22.5	1.7	15	Russia	19.9	1.8
16	Turkey	22.5	1.7	16	Turkey	17.4	1.6
17	South Korea	19.7	1.5	17	Norway	16.4	1.5
18	Romania	16.3	1.2	18	Sweden	16.1	1.5
19	Mexico	14.9	1.1	19	Romania	16.0	1.5
20	Slovakia	14.4	1.1	20	Slovakia	15.9	1.5
Sub-total		993.6	74.6			863.6	79.8
Germany Total		$1,330.0 bn	100.0%			$1,080.0 bn	100.0%

Source: MIT Observatory of Economic Complexity

While the US is Germany's primary export destination accounting for 8.4% of total exports, it is the source of only 5.7% of Germany's imports ranking fourth. Trade with France and the UK is similarly weighted in favour of German exports, but imports from China and the Netherlands outstrip exports.

In the context of the EU's post-Brexit trade negotiations, it is significant that German exports to the UK at $90.3 billion greatly exceeded its imports at $38.6 billion. It signals the task ahead for British exporters to achieve deeper penetration of German markets.

Canada does not feature as either a top 20 export market or import source. In light of the much lauded EU-Canada trade deal it will be interesting to see from 2019 onwards what the impact will be on Germany's trading pattern.

Appendix I.2 – Top 16 products of more than $100 million imported by Germany from the UK

Product	Import value $ billion	UK share exports (%)	Major Competitors Value of product imported ($bn)	All Total ($bn)
Motor cars	4.20	11.0	Sp(8.6), US(6.3), Cz(5.5), Me(4.1), It(3.9), Fr(3.7)	60.0
Aircraft parts	2.38	6.2	Fr(2.4), US(1.2), BL(0.4), Sp(0.3), Au(0.3), Tu(0.3)	8.6
Packaged medicaments	2.33	6.1	He(4.6), US(2.7), NL(2.5), It(2.1), Fr(2.1), Ir(2.1)	25.8
Crude petroleum	1.96	5.1	Ru(10.1), NL(4.1), No(3.1), Li(2.5), Kz(1.5), Ni(1.4)	30.1
Vehicle parts	1.22	3.2	Cz(6.0), Po(4.9), Fr(3.9), Ro(3.5), It(2.9), Au(6.6)	42.1
Platinum	1.00	2.6	No identified competitors	1.0
Broadcasting equipment	0.52	1.3	Ch(10.0), Vn(2.8), Cz(1.3), NL(1.2), OAS(0.5), Po(0.5)	20.9
Combustion engines	0.48	1.2	Au(1.6), Hu(1.3), Fr(0.4), Po(0.4), Sp(0.2), US(0.2)	5.0
Office machine parts	0.46	1.2	Ch(6.2), NL(1.5), Cz(1.2), SK(1.0), Th(0.9), Ph(0.9)	16.3
Spark-ignition engines	0.44	1.1	Hu(1.9), Au(1.0), Ro(0.1), Ja(0.1), US(0.1), Sp(0.1)	3.9
Centrifuges	0.43	1.1	SA(0.8), Ma(0.6), Cz(0.5), US(0.4), Fr(0.3), Au(0.3)	5.6
Human or animal blood	0.42	1.1	NL(6.7), US(4.3), He(3.7), Ir(1.4), BL(1.4), SK(1.1)	22.1

Hard liquor	0.39	1.0	It(0.2), US(0.2), Fr(0.2), Ir(0.1), Gr(0.1)	1.6
Medical instruments	0.35	0.9	US(2.2), He(0.8), Ja(0.6), NL(0.6), Ch(0.5), BL(0.3)	9.1
Laboratory reagents	0.33	0.8	US(1.3), Ja(0.3), Ir(0.2), NL(0.2), Fr(0.1), He(0.1)	2.9
Perfumes	0.32	0.8	Fr(0.8), It(0.2), Sp(0.1), He(0.1), NL(0.1), US(0.1)	1.7
Sub-total	17.63	44.7		256.7
TOTAL	$38.6 bn	100.0		$1,080 bn

Country key: *America(US), Australia(Aus), Austria(Au), Bahrein(BA), Benelux(BL), Canada(CA), Czech Rep.(Cz), France(Fr), Germany(D), Greece(Gr), Hong Kong(HK), Iraq(Irq), Rep. of Ireland(Ir), Italy(It), Japan(Ja), Kazakhstan(Kz), Libya(Li), Malaysia(Ma), Mexico(Me), Netherlands(NL), Nigeria(NI), Norway(No), Oman(Om), Other Asia (OAS), Philippines(Ph), Qatar(Q), Romania(Ro), Saudi Arabia(Sau), Singapore(Si), South Africa(SA), South Korea(SK), Sweden(Sw), Switzerland(He), Thailand(Th), Turkey(Tu), United Arab Emirates(UAE), United Kingdom (UK), Vietnam(Va)*

Source: MIT Observatory of Economic Complexity (OEC)

The UK's exports to Germany are highly diverse with the top 16 product categories accounting for less than 45% of the total. However, 26.5% of these exports are accounted for by motor cars, vehicle parts, aircraft parts and packaged medicaments (pharmaceuticals). The first three of these are vulnerable to the terms of the EU-UK trade arrangements under negotiation. The UK's automotive industry depends upon the free flow of components and sub-assemblies across the channel and the free export of finished goods to individual EU markets to be successful. Likewise, aircraft parts manufactured in the UK are sold into the Airbus programme in which the UK needs to maintain its status as a supplier.

Examining the detail of Appendix I.2 China is revealed as the primary UK competitor for broadcasting equipment and office machine parts and the US for medical instruments and laboratory reagents. Competition for other top 16 product categories is more dispersed. UK exports account for 3.6% of these 16 markets.

Note: In Appendix I.2 product group exports from competing countries of £50 million or less are not registered.

THE UNITED STATES OF AMERICA

Appendix II.1 – Top Import sources and export markets – 2017

Rank	Export market	$ billion	% of total	Rank	Import source	$ billion	% of total
1	Mexico	182.0	15.0	1	China	477.0	22.0
2	Canada	150.0	12.0	2	Mexico	307.0	14.0
3	China	133.0	11.0	3	Canada	275.0	13.0
4	Japan	66.9	5.3	4	Japan	125.0	5.8
5	Germany	61.6	4.9	5	Germany	112.0	5.2
6	South Korea	48.7	3.9	6	South Korea	69.4	3.2
7	UK	46.6	3.7	7	Vietnam	46.2	2.1
8	France	37.3	3.0	8	UK	45.2	2.1
9	Netherlands	35.2	2.8	9	Italy	45.0	2.1
10	Hong Kong	30.5	2.4	10	India	44.3	2.0
11	Belgium-Lux	29.4	2.3	11	Ireland	40.2	1.9
12	Singapore	24.3	1.9	12	France	36.0	1.7
13	India	22.8	1.8	13	Malaysia	33.1	1.5
14	Switzerland	21.3	1.7	14	Switzerland	28.4	1.3
15	Australia	20.5	1.6	15	Thailand	28.2	1.3
16	Brazil	20.4	1.6	16	Brazil	25.1	1.2
17	Ireland	17.3	1.4	17	Indonesia	19.9	0.9
18	Italy	16.6	1.3	18	Israel	18.2	0.8
19	Spain	14.9	1.2	19	Saudi Arabia	17.3	0.8
20	Malaysia	14.7	1.2	20	Singapore	16.6	0.8
Sub-total		994.0	80.0	Sub-total		1,809.1	84.5
America Total		$1,250.0 bn	100.0%	America Total		$2,160.0 bn	100.0%

Source: MIT Observatory of Economic Complexity

America's international trade is concentrated on its top 20 markets (80%) and countries of origin (84%). Imports outstrip exports by a ratio of 1.7 to 1. Its two trading partners in NAFTA, Canada and Mexico, account for 27% of both exports and imports, with China contributing 11% to total export and 22% of imports.

Among the remaining top 20, Germany, the UK and France are its major European partners with one important difference: at $112 billion German exports to the US were 1.8 times its imports, whereas UK exports at $45 billion were almost in balance with imports at $47 billion. France was in a similar position, with imports from the US at $37 billion only marginally greater than exports. Most other major partners had favourable trade balances with the US except for the Netherlands, whose imports of $35 billion were more than double its exports, Hong Kong, Belgium-Luxembourg, Ireland and Australia. Trade with Russia (imports at $15 billion) just failed to qualify within the top 20.

Developing export business with the US is notoriously difficult, demanding separate strategies and approaches at individual state levels. A UK-USA trade deal may not help greatly in taking market share from Mexico and Canada.

Appendix II.2 – Top 20 products of $300 million or more imported by the US from the UK

Product	Import value $ billion	UK share exports (%)	Major Competitors Value of product imported ($bn)	All Total ($bn)
Motor cars	8.81	19.0	CA(43.9), Ja(40.6), Me(30.0) D(21.7), SK(15.9), It(5.0)	170.0
Packaged medicaments	3.24	7.2	Ir(12.7), He(10.4), D(9.5), In(6.0), Is(4.0), Dk(3.0)	65.7
Refined petroleum	2.34	5.2	CA(9.9), Ru(6.5), SK(2.9), Al(2.5), In(2.4), NL(1.5)	46.3
Hard liquor	1.89	4.2	Fr(2.1), Me(1.3), Ir(0.6), Sw(0.3), CA(0.4), NL(0.3)	7.7
Aircraft parts	1.55	3.4	Ja(4.0), CA(2.1), Fr(1.5), Me(1.0), D(0.8), SK(0.7)	17.0
Human or animal blood	1.29	2.9	Ir(10.7), He(3.0), D(2.8), SK(1.3), It(1.2), BL(0.9)	26.2
Paintings	1.28	2.8	Fr(0.5), D(0.5), It(0.5), Sp(0.3), He(0.3), NL(0.3)	5.8
Gas turbines	0.76	1.7	CA(2.2), Si(1.6), D(0.9), Fr(0.8), La(0.1), It(0.1)	7.3
Seats	0.59	1.3	Ch(10.5), Me(10.5), CA(1.5), Vn(1.4), It(0.4), D(0.3)	23.9
Laboratory reagents	0.57	1.3	Si(0.4), D(0.4), CA(0.4), Ja(0.3), Sw(0.2), Fr(0.2)	3.3
Valves	0.47	1.0	Ch(3.9), Me(2.5), Ja(1.4), D(1.3), It(0.8), SK(0.5)	14.4
Spark ignition engines	0.45	1.0	Me(3.1), CA(2.3), Ja(2.0), D(1.6), Ch(0.6), Au(0.4)	11.2
Chemical analysis instruments	0.42	0.9	D(1.1), Ja(1.0), Si(0.7), Ch(0.6), Me(0.3), He(0.3)	6.1
Medical instruments	0.37	0.8	D(2.6), Me(2.5), Ja(1.8), Ir(1.7), Ch(1.6), Sw(1.2)	15.2

(Continued)

Appendix II.2 – (Continued)

Product	Import value $ billion	UK share exports (%)	Major Competitors Value of product imported ($bn)	All Total ($bn)
Vehicle parts	0.35	0.8	Me(23.0), Ch(10.0), CA(9.0), Ja(8.3), D(5.0), SK(4.2)	67.1
Centrifuges	0.35	0.8	Me(2.0), Ch(1.3), D(1.0), CA(0.8), Ja(0.5), SK(0.2)	8.1
Delivery trucks	0.34	0.7	Me(22.8), CA(1.7), Ja(0.8), D(0.4), Sp(0.3), Sw(0.1)	26.7
Large construction vehicles	0.34	0.7	Ja(3.0), Br(0.7), SK(0.5), D(0.3), Ch(0.2), Fr(0.2)	6.0
Liquid pumps	0.33	0.7	Ch(2.2), Me(1.6), D(1.1), CA(1.1), Ja(1.0), It(0.4)	10.1
Electrical control boards	0.31	0.7	Me(4.3), Ch(1.7), D(0.9), C(0.8), Ja(0.7), Si(0.3)	11.3
Sub-total	26.05	57.6		284.1
TOTAL	$45.20 bn	100.0		$1,080.0 bn

Country key: *Algeria(Al), America(US), Australia(Aus), Austria(Au), Bahrein(BR), Benelux(BL), Canada(CA), Denmark(Dk), Czech Rep.(Cz), France(Fr), Germany(D), Hong Kong(HK), India(In), Iraq(Iq), Rep. of Ireland(Ir), Israel(Is), Italy(It), Japan(Ja), Kazakhstan(Kz), Latvia(la), Libya(Li), Malaysia(Ma), Mexico(Me), Netherlands(NL), Nigeria(NI), Norway(No), Oman(Om), Other Asia (OAS), Qatar(Q), Poland(Po), Russia(Ru) Saudi Arabia(Sau), Singapore(Si), South Korea(SK), Sweden(Sw), Switzerland(He), Thailand(Th), Turkey(Tu), United Arab Emirates(UAE), United Kingdom(UK), United States of America(US), Vietnam(Vn)*

Source: MIT Observatory of Economic Complexity (OEC)

The top 20 product groups account for nearly 58% of the UK's total exports to the USA, but just 9% of total US imports of those product groups. However, this concentration of leading products compares favourably with the UK's overall share of global exports to the US which amounted to only 4.2%.

Comparison with Germany highlights the challenge for British exporters. Excluding motor cars, UK exports of its top product groups to the US were $17.24 billion compared with more than $30 billion of the same products from Germany. A favourable Anglo-American trade deal may help to address the challenge.

NETHERLANDS

Appendix III.1 – Top 20 Import sources and export markets – 2017

Rank	Export market	$ billion	% of total	Rank	Import source	$ billion	% of total
1	Germany	89.9	19.0	1	Germany	84.5	17.0
2	Belgium-Lux.	67.6	15.0	2	Belgium-Lux.	49.3	10.0
3	UK	47.0	10.0	3	China	43.9	9.0
4	France	29.8	6.4	4	US	35.2	7.2
5	Italy	24.8	5.4	5	UK	24.9	5.1
6	US	16.4	3.5	6	France	18.3	5.1
7	China	11.9	2.6	7	Italy	11.5	2.4
8	Sweden	11.9	2.6	8	Japan	9.6	2.0
9	Poland	8.7	1.9	9	Spain	9.4	1.9
10	Denmark	6.7	1.4	10	Poland	9.4	1.9
11	South Korea	6.3	1.4	11	Norway	7.9	1.6
12	Switzerland	5.2	1.1	12	Sweden	7.6	1.6
13	Singapore	5.1	1.1	13	Brazil	7.6	1.6
14	Hungary	4.8	1.0	14	Malaysia	7.4	1.5
15	Austria	4.8	1.0	15	Ireland	6.4	1.3
16	Czech Republic	4.7	1.0	16	Hong Kong	6.1	1.3
17	Russia	4.7	1.0	17	Vietnam	6.0	1.3
18	Turkey	4.2	0.9	18	Czech Republic	5.8	1.2
19	Finland	3.8	0.8	19	Singapore	5.5	1.1
20	Norway	3.6	0.8	20	Finland	4.6	1.0
Sub-total		351.9	77.9			353.7	74.5
Netherlands Total		$462.0 bn	100.0%			$485.0 bn	100.0%

Source: MIT Observatory of Economic Complexity

Excluding the UK, the top 5 of the Netherland's exports in 2017 were to other EU members at 46% of the total. The UK accounted for a further 10%. Beyond the top 5, the US and China accounted for the next 6%. Among the remaining export markets in the top 20, only South Korea, Singapore, Russia and Turkey were beyond Europe, together contributing only 4.4% to exports. These 20 markets together were the destinations for 78% of the Netherlands' total exports.

The Netherlands maintains a reasonable balance in its international merchandise trade with imports at $485 billion, some $23 billion more than exports in 2017. Germany and Belgium-Luxembourg are the first two countries of origin for imports. The Netherlands imported slightly less than it exported to Germany and substantially less in its trade with the latter. However, imports from China and the US, which rank next together account for $79 billion (16% of total imports), both outpace exports by more than 3.5 and twice respectively. Conversely, exports to the UK were almost double imports.

More often than not, exports to most other European countries from the Netherlands exceed imports. In the case of Denmark, Switzerland, Hungary and Austria, which rank among the top 20 export destinations, none of the four appear in the top 20 countries of origin.

Appendix III.2 – Top 20 products of more than $100 million imported by Netherlands from the UK

Product	Import value $ billion	UK share exports (%)	Major Competitors Value of product imported ($bn)	All Total ($bn)
Crude petroleum	4.42	18.0	Ru(14.2), No(3.8), Iq(2.8), Kz(2.4), Ku(1.8), Nl(1.7)	36.4
Refined Petroleum	3.02	12.0	Ru(8.3), BL(5.4), UK(3.0), Fr(1.5), Sp(1.1), Sw(1.1)	33.1
Packaged medicaments	1.16	4.7	D(3.1), BL(0.8), He(0.7), US(0.6), Fr(0.5), It(0.4)	9.2
Motor cars	0.77	3.1	D(3.6), BL(2.5), Sp(0.6), Fr(0.6), Cz(0.5), SK(0.3)	10.6
Petroleum gas	0.68	2.7	No(0.5), BL(0.4), US(0.3), Sp(0.1)	2.2
Broadcasting equipment	0.52	2.1	Ch(6.1), US(2.1), HK(1.9), D(0.9), Vn(0.8), Cz(0.7)	17.8
Gas turbines	0.35	1.4	US(0.8), C(0.2), Fr(0.2), Hu(0.1), SK(0.1), HK(0.1)	2.6
Coal tar oil	0.32	1.3	BL(0.9), D(0.4), Sp(0.3), Fr(0.2), Ru(0.2), Al(0.2)	3.4
Industrial printers	0.31	1.2	Ja(1.2), D(1.2), Ch(0.8), Fr(0.2), US(0.1), Ma(0.1)	4.8
Office machine parts	0.30	1.2	Ch(5.1), Ma(2.6), Vn(1.4), Th(0.9), Ja(0.8), D(0.7)	15.9
Amine compounds	0.26	1.1	Sp(0.2), Fr(0.1)	0.6
Delivery trucks	0.25	1.0	D(0.9), BL(0.6), Sp(0.2), Fr(0.2), Po(0.2), Sp(0.2)	2.8
Photographic chemicals	0.25	1.0	*All competitors less than $100 mn*	0.4
Vehicle parts	0.23	0.9	D(1.7), Sw(0.9), BL(0.8), Ja(0.5), Po(0.3), Fr(0.2)	6.0

Acylic hydrocarbons	0.19	0.8	BL(0.4), D(0.2), Ru(0.1), Sp(0.1), Fr(0.1), It(0.1)	1.3
Spark-ignition engines	0.18	0.7	Au(0.1)	0.4
Orthopaedic appliances	0.18	0.7	US(1.8), Ir(0.8), Fr(0.6), D(0.5), Si(0.4), He(0.4)	5.6
Computers	0.18	0.7	Ch(5.3), HK(1.0), US(0.9), D(0.8), Cz(0.6), BL(0.5)	11.0
Hard liquor	0.15	0.6	D(0.2), BL(0.1), Fr(0.1), US(0.1)	0.8
Air pumps	0.14	0.6	D(0.4), Th(0.2), Ja(0.1), BL(0.1), Ch(0.1), It(0.1)	1.5
Sub-total	13.95	55.8		166.0
TOTAL	$24.9 bn	100.0		$485 bn

Country key: America(US), Australia(Aus), Austria(Au), Bahrein(BA), Benelux(BL), Canada(CA), Czech Rep.(Cz), France(Fr), Germany(D), Hong Kong(HK), Iraq(Irq), Rep. of Ireland(Ir), Italy(It), Japan(Ja), Kazakhstan(Kz), Kuwait(Ku), Libya(Li), Malaysia(Ma), Mexico(Me), Netherlands(NL), Nigeria(NI), Norway(No), Oman(Om), Other Asia (OAS), Qatar(Q), Saudi Arabia(Sau), Singapore(Si), South Korea(SK), Sweden(Sw), Switzerland(He), Thailand(Th), Turkey(Tu), United Arab Emirates(UAE), United Kingdom UK), Vietnam(Va)

Source: MIT Observatory of Economic Complexity (OEC)

Although the top 20 product groups in UK exports to the Netherlands account for 56% of trade, the total is skewed by exports of crude and refined petroleum, and petroleum gas which contribute nearly 33%. In the long term this major element of the UK's exports will be unsustainable, as North Sea oil and gas is depleted and the market for petroleum products eroded by movement away from carbon fuels, so that UK exporters should focus on the 17 other product groups which together contributed $16.8 billion in 2017.

Among these Germany, Belgium Luxembourg and China form the dominant competition, with the US as the leading supplier in gas turbines and orthopaedic appliances. UK exports are highly diverse with many other products accounting for less than $140 million in annual sales. It may be that for new exporters the Netherlands offers suitable market opportunities to gain experience.

Note: In Appendix III.2 product group exports from competing countries of $50 million or less are not registered.

FRANCE

Appendix IV.1 – Top 20 Import sources and export markets – 2017

Rank	Export market	$ billion	% of total	Rank	Import source	$ billion	% of total
1	Germany	69.1	13.0	1	Germany	104.0	17.0
2	Italy	39.7	7.7	2	China	52.9	8.9
3	Belgium-Lux.	39.7	7.7	3	Italy	48.0	8.1
4	Spain	37.6	7.3	4	Belgium-Lux.	44.6	7.5
5	UK	36.0	7.0	5	Spain	40.5	6.8
6	US	36.0	7.0	6	US	37.3	6.3
7	China	22.2	4.3	7	Netherlands	29.8	5.0
8	Netherlands	18.3	3.5	8	UK	24.8	4.2
9	Switzerland	16.4	3.2	9	Switzerland	15.3	2.6
10	Japan	9.3	1.8	10	Poland	11.7	2.0
11	Poland	8.9	1.7	11	Czech Republic	8.4	1.4
12	Singapore	7.5	1.5	12	Turkey	8.0	1.4
13	Ireland	7.5	1.5	13	Ireland	7.6	1.3
14	Russia	7.5	1.4	14	Norway	7.5	1.3
15	Hong Kong	6.5	1.3	15	Portugal	6.9	1.2
16	South Korea	6.4	1.2	16	Sweden	6.6	1.1
17	Sweden	5.8	1.1	17	Russia	6.1	1.0
18	Portugal	5.7	1.1	18	India	5.8	1.0
19	India	5.2	1.0	19	Vietnam	5.8	1.0
20	Algeria	5.1	1.0	20	Austria	5.6	0.9
Sub-total		395.4	75.3	Sub-total		477.2	80.0
France Total		$517 bn	100.0%	France Total		$595 bn	100.0%

Source: MIT Observatory of Economic Complexity

Among its top 5 trade partners only the UK imported more from than it exported to France in a ratio of nearly 3:2. Notably, Germany and China had merchandise trade surpluses with France of 50% and 138% respectively. The gap of $82 billion in trade with France's top 20 partners reflects its overall gap in its total trade of $78 billion.

Japan, Singapore, Hong Kong, South Korea and Algeria feature among the top 20 export destinations but not among the top 20 country origins of imports. Conversely, the Czech Republic, Turkey, Vietnam and Austria are listed as top 20 countries of origin but do not appear in the top 20 list of export destinations, and these will be markets where French exporters will seek to improve penetration.

Appendix IV.2 – Top 20 products of more than $100 million imported by France from the UK

Product	Import value $ billion	UK share exports (%)	Major Competitors Value of product imported ($bn)	All Total ($bn)
Motor cars	2.09	8.5	D(9.9), Sp(6.4), Sl(2.1), Tu(1.8), It(1.7), BL(1.4)	35.1
Aircraft parts	1.95	7.9	US(7.0), D(0.7), Sp(0.), Ch(0.4), Ca(0.4), BL(0.3)	12.5
Crude petroleum	0.71	2.9	Kz(3.1), Sa(2.4), Ir(2.3), Ru(2.3), Al(2.1), Ni(2.0)	20.6
Hard liquor	0.69	2.8	US(0.1), Po(0.1), It(0.1)	
Packaged medicaments	0.69	2.8	D(2.4), US(2.0), Ir(1.7), It(1.2), NL(0.7), Sp(0.6)	14.2
Vehicle parts	0.60	2.4	D(3.4), Sp(1.6), It(1.4), Cz(0.9), Ja(0.9), Po(0.6)	14.9
Refined petroleum	0.49	2.0	NL(2.1), US(1.9), Ru(1.9), BL(1.7), Sp(1.1), D(0.9)	16.7
Human or animal blood	0.41	1.6	D(1.4), US(1.1), BL(1.0), He(1.0), Ir(0.3), It(0.2)	6.1
Broadcasting equipment	0.32	1.3	Ch(5.9), Vn(1.7), NL(0.5), US(0.5), Me(0.3), D(0.3)	11.3
Office machine parts	0.21	0.8	Ch(1.9), NL(0.6), D(0.5), Th(0.4), Ja(0.3), US(0.2)	5.5
Hormones	0.17	0.7	US(0.7), BL(0.4), Ir(0.1)	1.6
Fork-lifts	0.16	0.6	D(0.5), It(0.3), Ch(0.1)	1.2
Large construction vehicles	0.16	0.6	D(0.3), Ja(0.2), NL(0.1), BL(0.1), Au(0.1), Sp(0.1)	1.5
Laboratory reagents	0.15	0.6	US(0.5), D(0.3), Ir(0.1), NL(0.1), Ja(0.1), Sw(0.1)	1.5

(Continued)

Appendix IV.2 – (Continued)

Product	Import value $ billion	UK share exports (%)	Major Competitors Value of product imported ($bn)	All Total ($bn)
Cleaning products	0.15	0.6	D(0.4), BL(0.3), It(0.3), NL(0.2), Sp(0.1), Po(0.1)	1.7
Tractors	0.15	0.6	D(1.0), NL(0.5), BL(0.4), It(0.3), Tu(0.1), Ja(0.1)	3.0
Excavation machinery	0.14	0.6	D(0.6), It(0.4), Sw(0.2), BL(0.1), NL(0.1), Sp(0.1)	2.5
Centrifuges	0.14	0.6	D(0.6), US(0.4), It(0.2), Po(0.1), Sp(0.1), Ch(0.1)	2.4
Medical instruments	0.14	0.6	US(1.1), D(0.7), NL(0.4), He(0.2), Ja(0.2), BL(0.2)	4.6
Sub-total	9.52	38.5		148.3
TOTAL	$24.8 bn	100.0		$595 bn

Country key: America(US), Australia(Aus), Austria(Au), Bahrein(BA), Benelux(BL), Canada(CA), Czech Rep.(Cz), France(Fr), Germany(D), Hong Kong(HK), Iraq(Irq), Rep. of Ireland(Ir), Italy(It), Japan(Ja), Kazakhstan(Kz), Libya(Li), Malaysia(Ma), Mexico(Me), Netherlands(Nl), Nigeria(NI), Norway(No), Oman(Om), Other Asia (OAS), Poland(Po), Qatar(Q), Saudi Arabia(Sau), Singapore(Si), Slovakia(Sl) Korea(SK), Sweden(Sw), Switzerland(He), Thailand(Th), Turkey(Tu), United Arab Emirates(UAE), United Kingdom (UK), Vietnam(Va)

Source: MIT Observatory of Economic Complexity (OEC)

Motor cars, vehicle parts and aircraft parts total 18.8% of the UK's exports to France, with crude and refined petroleum recording a further 4.9%. Therefore exports of other products are limited to less than $19 billion.

Reviewing competition, Germany is the major supplier for 10 out of the UK's top 20 export categories, with the US accounting for a further five and China for two. The UK's share of French imports in the top 20 categories is 6.4% against 4.2% for all merchandise. As is the case with Germany and the Netherlands, it is clear that UK exporters have a major challenge in increasing market penetration across the board with or without continuing alignment of standards.

Note: In Appendix IV.2 product group exports from competing countries of $50 million or less are not registered.

CHINA
Appendix V.1 – Top Import sources and export markets – 2017

Rank	Export market	$ billion	% of total	Rank	Import source	$ billion	% of total
1	United States	477.0	20.0	1	Other Asia	151.0	9.8
2	Hong Kong	256.0	11.0	2	South Korea	150.0	9.7
3	Japan	157.0	6.5	2	Japan	136.0	8.8
4	Germany	109.0	4.5	4	United States	133.0	8.7
5	South Korea	98.1	4.1	5	Germany	95.0	6.2
6	Vietnam	70.6	2.9	6	Australia	85.0	5.5
7	India	68.8	2.9	7	Singapore	50.3	3.3
5	UK	58.9	2.4	5	Brazil	48.0	3.1
6	France	52.9	2.2	6	Malaysia	42.5	2.8
7	Mexico	52.1	2.2	7	Thailand	40.7	2.6
8	Canada	50.0	2.1	8	Vietnam	39.9	2.6
9	Australia	47.0	1.9	9	Russia	39.1	2.5
10	Netherlands	43.9	1.8	10	Saudi Arabia	29.1	1.9
11	Russia	43.8	1.8	11	Switzerland	26.1	1.7
12	Malaysia	38.1	1.6	12	France	22.2	1.4
13	Spain	28.6	1.2	13	UK	21.9	1.4
14	UAE	28.6	1.2	14	Philippines	20.0	1.3
15	Brazil	27.1	1.1	15	Iran	16.9	1.1
16	Poland	25.9	1.1	16	Italy	16.4	1.1
17	Turkey	23.0	0.9	17	Hong Kong	16.4	1.1
Sub-total		1,738.4	73.4	Sub-total		1,182.5	75.9
China Total		$2,410.0	100.0%	China Total		$1,540.0	100.0%

Source: MIT Observatory of Economic Complexity

China sourced 42% of its 2017 imports from other Asian countries, with South Korea and Japan as its two largest partners together accounting for 18.5%. Its third largest single source of imports was the US (8.7%) followed by Germany (6.2%) and Australia (5.5%). The next European sources were Switzerland (1.7%), then France and the UK (1.4% each). The challenge for UK industry is to raise exports towards Germany's performance, which is more than four times the UK level. Appendix V.2 provides some insight as to how the UK competes with Germany in its main product categories.

In terms of its balance of trade China's exports to the US are more than three times its imports, indicating how severely the Chinese economy was affected in 2019 by their trade and will continue to be impacted in 2020 by the coronavirus pandemic. At lower levels UK and French imports from China exceeded exports by rather less than 3 to 1 while Germany's trade was almost in balance.

Appendix V.2 – Top 16 products of more than $100 million imported by China from the UK

Product	Import value $ billion	UK share exports (%)	Major Competitors Value of product imported ($bn)	All Total ($bn)
Motor cars	6.04	28.0	D(13.6), US(11.5), Ja(6.7), It(1.8), SK(1.2), Sw(0.7)	46.8
Crude petroleum	3.62	17.0	Ru(20.7), Sau(18.5), An(18.0), Irq(12.5), Om(11.2), Irn(10.8)	145.0
Packaged medicaments	1.15	5.3	D(2.2), HE(1.9), US(1.4), Sw(1.1), Fr(1.0), It(0.8)	14.2
Recovered paper	0.51	2.3	US((2.0), Ja(0.5), NL(0.2), HK(0.2), It(0.2), Sp(0.1)	4.6
Scrap copper	0.46	2.1	US(1.6), HK(1.5), Ja(0.7), Au(0.6), D(0.5), Th(0.4)	8.9
Gold	0.45	2.0	He(14.8), Aus(8.8), SA(7.1), Si(4.7); US(2.7), CA((0.3)	40.3
Gas turbines	0.40	1.8	US(1.8), Fr(1.4), HK(1.2), Ru(1.1), D(0.3), It(0.2)	7.3
Vehicle parts	0.34	1.5	D(9.5), Ja(7.2), SK(2.8), US(2.1), BL(0.5), Me(0.5)	26.7
Chemical analysis instruments	0.26	1.2	US(1.8), D(1.1), Ja(1.0), Si(0.9), He(0.1), Fr(0.1)	6.4
Aircraft parts	0.24	1.1	D(0.7), US(0.7), Fr(0.3), Si(0.1), Ma(0.1), SK(0.1)	2.4
Combustion engines	0.23	1.1	US(1.8), Fr(1.4), HK(1.2), Ru(1.1); D(0.3), It(0.2)	7.3
Other measuring instruments	0.23	1.1	D(1.7), Ja(1.4), SK(1.2), US(0.8), OAS(0.7), Ma(0.2)	8.3
Human and animal blood	0.15	0.7	He(1.4), US(1.4), D(1.0), Ir(0.4), Fr(0.3), Au(0.2), BL(0.2)	5.7

Beauty products	0.12	0.5	SK(1.4), Ja(0.9), Fr(0.8), US(0.4); He(0.1), S(0.1)	4.6
Engine parts	0.11	0.5	D(1.1), Ja(0.9), US(0.4), SK(0.4), It(0.1), Th(0.1)	3.7
Laboratory reagents	0.11	0.5	US(0.7), D(0.3), Ja(0.2), Fr(0.1), Si(0.1)	1.7
Lcds	0.10	0.5	OAS(10.9), SK(9.9), Ja(4.5), Th(1.7), Vn(1.4), D(0.6)	30.2
Hard liquor	0.10	0.5	Fr(0.6), Si(0.2), HK(0.1), Aus(0.1), Ja(0.1)	1.2
Sub-total	14.46	66.0		364.3
TOTAL	$22 bn	100.0		$1,540 bn

Country key: America(US), Angola(An), Australia(Aus), Austria(Au), Bahrein(BA), Benelux(BL), Canada(CA), Czech Rep. (Cz), France(Fr), Germany(D), Hong Kong(HK), Iran(Irn), Iraq(Irq), Rep. of Ireland(Ir), Italy(It), Japan(Ja), Malaysia(Ma), Mexico(Me), Netherlands(NL), Norway(No), Oman(Om), Other Asia (OAS), Qatar(Q), Saudi Arabia(Sau), Russia(RU), Singapore(Si), South Korea(SK), Sweden(Sw), Switzerland(He), Thailand(T), Turkey(Tu), United Arab Emirates(UAE), United Kingdom (UK), Vietnam(Va)

Source: MIT Observatory of Economic Complexity (OEC)

Appendix V.2 reveals that the top 16 UK product groups accounted for just 66% of its exports of goods to China, whereas China's total imports of the same products amounting to \$364 billion accounted for less than 24% of China's annual imports. The US and Germany are confirmed as the UK's strongest competitors, each ranking as leading supplier 6 times and in second place twice.

Note: In Appendix V.2 product group exports from competing countries of \$50 million or less are not registered.

JAPAN
Appendix VI.1 – Top 20 Import sources and export markets – 2017

Rank	Export market	$ billion	% of total	Rank	Import source	$ billion	% of total
1	China	136.0	20.0	1	China	157.0	25.0
2	US	125.0	18.0	2	US	66.9	11.0
3	South Korea	54.2	7.3	3	Australia	34.6	5.5
4	Other Asia	32.9	4.7	4	Saudi Arabia	25.0	4.0
5	Hong Kong	32.1	4.6	5	Other Asia	23.0	3.6
6	Thailand	26.2	3.8	6	Germany	22.5	3.6
7	Germany	24.5	3.5	7	Thailand	22.0	3.5
8	Singapore	17.5	2.5	8	Indonesia	19.0	3.0
9	Australia	16.3	2.3	9	UAE	18.8	3.0
10	Mexico	14.8	2.1	10	Vietnam	18.1	2.9
11	UK	14.5	2.1	11	Malaysia	17.8	2.8
12	Indonesia	13.5	1.9	12	Singapore	12.2	1.9
13	Malaysia	13.4	1.9	13	Russia	11.8	1.9
14	Vietnam	13.1	1.9	14	Philippines	11.4	1.8
15	Canada	11.7	1.7	15	Qatar	10.0	1.6
16	Phillippines	11.6	1.7	16	Canada	9.7	1.5
17	France	10.6	1.5	17	France	9.4	1.5
18	Belgium-Lux.	9.8	1.4	18	Italy	8.4	1.3
19	Netherlands	9.6	1.4	19	Switzerland	7.6	1.2
20	India	9.3	1.3	20	UK	7.1	1.1
Sub-total		539.6	76.6			511.5	81.7
Japan Total		$695 bn	100.0%			$633 bn	100.0%

Source: MIT Observatory of Economic Complexity

Japan's dominant top 2 trading partners are China and the US, together accounting for 38% of exports and 36% of 2017 total imports in 2017. The next four export markets are all in East Asia, contributing another 19.6%, and a further five add another 9.9% to the export total.

Import sources are more diverse, with Australia in third and Saudi Arabia (Japan's primary supplier of oil) in fourth places. Germany in sixth place is the leading European exporter to Japan with sales at $22.5 billion, only $2 billion less than imports. In contrast, UK exports at $7.1 billion were less than half its imports, accounting for 1.1% of Japan's total imports against Germany's share of 3.6%. Import shares of France, Italy and Switzerland at 1.5% and less were all ahead of the UK, with France's trade deficit only $1.2 billion and the latter two in surplus.

The UK's first step towards gaining an increased market share is signature of its FTA with Japan at the beginning of 2021.

Appendix VI.2 – Top 20 products of more than $50 million imported by Japan from the UK

Product	Import value $ billion	UK share exports (%)	Major Competitors Value of product imported ($bn)	All Total ($bn)
Packaged medicaments	1.20	17.0	US(2.3), D(1.9), He(1.5), Fr(1.3), Si(1.0), Ir(0.1)	14.0
Motor cars	1.16	16.0	D(5.6), US(0.8), It(0.7), SA(0.7), BL(0.3), NL(0.3)	11.4
Gas turbines	0.56	7.9	US(2.3), It(0.1), HK(01), D(0.1), Hu(0.1), Ch(0.1)	6.3
Hard liquor	0.24	3.4	US(0.1), SK(0.1), Fr(0.1)	0.7
Combustion engines	0.15	2.2	D(0.3), Fr(0.2), It(0.2), SK(0.1), Th(0.1)	1.0
Platinum	0.12	1.7	Sa(2.5), Ru(0.6), He(0.1), D(0.1), US(0.1), OAS(0.1)	3.6
Laboratory reagents	0.09	1.3	US(0.3), SW(0.1), D(0.1)	0.6
Chemical analysis instruments	0.09	1.3	US(0.5), D(0.2), Ch(0.2), Si(0.1)	1.4
Vehicle parts	0.08	1.2	Ch(3.0), Th(0.8), SK(0.7), US(0.5), Me(0.5), Vn(0.4)	8.3
Radioactive chemicals	0.07	1.1	US(0.1)	0.3
Thermostats	0.07	1.1	Ch(0.5), US(0.4), D(0.3), Th(0.2), Ph(0.1)	1.9
Aircraft parts	0.07	1.0	US(1.2), SK(0.3), Ca(0.1), Ma(0.1), Fr(0.1)	2.0
Optical fibres	0.07	1.0	Ir(0.6), US(0.5), Ch(0.4), OA(0.2), D(0.1), Si(0.1)	2.4
Centrifuges	0.06	0.8	Ch(0.4), US(0.3), D(0.2), SK(0.1), Th(0.1), Fr(0.1)	1.5
Medical instruments	0.06	0.8	US(2.2), CH(0.6), D(0.4), Me(0.4), Ir(0.3), Cr(0.3)	5.7
Beauty products	0.05	0.8	Fr(0.4), US(0.2), SK(0.2), Ch(0.1)	1.1
Electric motors	0.05	0.8	Ch(0.9), Vn(0.2), Th(0.1), US(0.1), SK(0.1), Ph(0.1)	1.8

(Continued)

183

Appendix VI.2 – (Continued)

Product	Import value $ billion	UK share exports (%)	Major Competitors Value of product imported ($bn)	All Total ($bn)
Engine parts	0.05	0.7	Ch(0.4), US(0.3), Th(0.2), SK(0.1), Id(0.1), D(0.1)	1.8
Special function machinery	0.05	0.7	US(0.9), Ch(0.8), D(0.3), OA(0.2), Si(0.1), Ma(0.1)	3.6
Human or animal blood	0.05	0.7	US(2.0), He(1.3), D(1.2), Ir(0.7), Fr(0.1), BL(0.1)	5.9
Sub-total	4.34	61.4		77.3
TOTAL	$7.07 bn	100.0		$633 bn

Country key: *America(US), Australia(Aus), Austria(Au), Bahrein(BA), Benelux(BL), Canada(CA), China(Ch), Costa Rica(Cr), Czech Rep.(Cz), France(Fr), Germany(D), Hong Kong(HK), Iraq(Irq), Italy(It), Japan(Ja), Kazakhstan(Kz), Libya(Li), Malaysia(Ma), Mexico(Me), Netherlands(NL), Nigeria(NI), Norway(No), Oman(Om), Other Asia (OAS), Philippines(Ph), Poland(Po), Qatar(Q), Russia(Ru), Saudi Arabia(Sau), Singapore(Si), Slovakia(Sl), South Korea(SK), South Africa(SA), Sweden(Sw), Switzerland(He), Thailand(Th), Turkey(Tu), United Arab Emirates(UAE), United Kingdom (UK), Vietnam(Vn)*

Source: MIT Observatory of Economic Complexity (OEC)

Note: In Appendix VI.2 product group exports from competing countries of $50 million or less are not registered.

Table VI.2 highlights the weakness of the UK's penetration into Japanese markets. top 20 product group exports at $4.3 billion account for 61% of its total exports to Japan, and these products represent 77% of Japan's total imports. The US is the dominant supplier for 10 of these 20 markets and Germany has gained a foothold as lead supplier in 2 categories and second or third source for 7 more. France is lead supplier of beauty products and the UK for hard liquor, but these are both minor Japanese markets for imports.

SOUTH KOREA

Appendix VII.1 – Top 20 Import sources and export markets – 2017

Rank	Export market	$ billion	% of total	Rank	Import source	$ billion	% of total
1	China	150.0	25.0	1	China	98.1	21.0
2	US	69.4	12.0	2	Japan	54.2	11.0
3	Hong Kong	34.8	5.8	3	US	48.7	10.0
4	Japan	26.3	4.5	4	Germany	19.7	4.2
5	Australia	18.7	3.1	5	Australia	18.0	3.8
6	Singapore	18.1	3.1	6	Vietnam	16.1	3.4
7	India	15.3	2.6	7	Singapore	14.2	3.0
8	Other Asia	14.9	2.5	8	Qatar	10.3	2.2
9	Mexico	10.9	1.8	9	Indonesia	9.2	2.0
10	Germany	12.0	2.0	10	UAE	8.9	1.9
11	UK	9.2	1.5	11	Kuwait	8.7	1.8
12	Philippines	8.7	1.5	12	Malaysia	8.0	1.7
13	Malaysia	8.2	1.4	13	Iran	7.2	1.5
14	Indonesia	8.0	1.3	14	UK	6.6	1.4
15	Thailand	7.5	1.3	15	France	6.4	1.4
16	Russia	7.2	1.2	16	Netherlands	6.3	1.3
17	Marshall Islands	6.9	1.2	17	Iraq	5.7	1.2
18	Turkey	6.4	1.2	18	Italy	5.4	1.2
19	Norway	5.7	1.0	19	India	5.0	1.1
20	Brazil	5.4	0.9	20	Canada	4.6	0.9
Sub-total		443.6	74.9	Sub-total		361.4	76.7
South Korea Total		$597 bn	100.0%	South Korea Total		$471 bn	100.0%

Source: MIT Observatory of Economic Complexity

South Korea maintained a comfortable trade surplus in merchandise ($126 billion in 2017). Exports to the first 7 of its top 20 destinations except for Japan, whose exports to South Korea were more than double its imports. However, imports from Germany, Vietnam, Qatar, UAE, Kuwait, Indonesia, France, Iran, Iraq, Italy and Canada were greater than exports of these only Indonesia was among the top 20. The top 5 countries of origin for imported merchandise: China, Japan, the US, Germany and Australia together accounted for 50% of all South Korea's imports. Germany accounted for more than 4 per cent, while the UK, France and the Netherlands were the only other European country suppliers, each capturing less than 1.5% of the market.

Appendix VII.2 – Top 20 products of more than $30 million imported by South Korea from the UK

Product	Import value $ billion	UK share exports (%)	Major Competitors Value of product imported ($bn)	All Total ($bn)
Crude petroleum	2.01	30.0	Sau(15.3), KU(7.5), Irn(7.0), Irq(5.7), UAE(4.6), Ru(3.9)	56.0
Motor cars	0.94	14.0	D(4.6), US(1.6), Ja(1.1), Au(0.4), It(0.3), Sp(0.2)	9.8
Packaged medicaments	0.18	2.8	D(0.6), US(0.6), He(0.3), Ir(0.2), Ja(0.2), It(0.2)	3.2
Gas turbines	0.15	2.3	US(1.0), Ja(0.2), D(0.1), NL(0.1), Fr(0.1)	1.7
Hard liquor	0.14	2.1	No competition of $50 million or more	0.2
Combustion engines	0.14	2.1	Ja(0.3), Fr(0.2), D(0.1), Sw(0.1), Hu(0.1), It(0.1)	1.2
Radioactive chemicals	0.14	2.1	Kz(0.3), Ru(0.3), NL(0.2), D(0.1), Aus(0.1), US(0.1)	1.3
Platinum	0.13	1.9	Ru(0.2), SA(0.1), Ja(0.1)	0.6
Paintings	0.10	1.5	US(0.1)	0.3
Chemical analysis instruments	0.08	1.2	US(0.5), Ja(0.5), D(0.3), Ch(0.1), Vn(0.1), Is(0.1)	1.9
Valves	0.07	1.1	Ch(0.5), Ja(0.5), US(0.4), D(0.2), It(0.2), Fr(0.1)	2.4
Silicone	0.06	1.0	Ch(0.1), Ja(0.1), US(0.1)	0.5
Other measuring instruments	0.06	1.0	US(0.5), Ja(0.4), D(0.3), Si(0.2), Ch(0.2), Vn(0.1)	2.5
Planes, helicopters, spacecraft	0.06	1.0	US(1.2), Fr(0.8), D(0.1)	2.2

Functional machinery	0.06	0.9	Ja(3.9), US(1.5), Si(0.6), Ch(0.5), D(0.5), NL(0.3)	9.0
Centrifuges	0.05	0.7	US(0.3), D(0.2), Ch(0.2), Ja(0.2)	1.4
Liquid pumps	0.05	0.7	Ja(0.3), D(0.3), US(0.2), Ch(0.2), Cz(0.1), It(0.1)	1.5
Aircraft parts	0.05	0.5	US(0.5), Fr(0.1), Is(0.1)	0.9
Oscilloscopes	0.03	0.5	Ja(0.5), US(0.4), Ch(0.2), Ma(0.2), D(0.1),	1.5
Vehicle parts	0.03	0.5	Ch(1.1), Ja(0.8), D(0.5), US(0.3), Me(0.2), Fr(0.2)	3.9
Sub-total	4.53	67.9		102.0
TOTAL	$6.59 bn	100.0		$471 bn

Country key: *America(US), Australia(Aus), Austria(Au), Bahrein(BA), Benelux(BL), Canada(CA), Costa Rica(Cr), Czech Rep.(Cz), France(Fr), Germany(D), Hong Kong(HK), Iran(Irn), Iraq(Irq), Rep. of Ireland(Ir), Israel(Is), Italy(It), Japan(Ja), Kazakhstan(Kz), Libya(Li), Malaysia(Ma), Mexico(Me), Netherlands(NL), Nigeria(NI), Norway(No), Oman(Om), Other Asia (OAS), Phillippines(ph), Poland(Po), Qatar(Q), Russia(Ru), Saudi Arabia(Sau), Singapore(Si), Slovakia(Sl) South Korea(SK) South Africa(SA), Sweden(Sw), Switzerland(He), Thailand(Th), Turkey(Tu), United Arab Emirates(UAE), United Kingdom (UK), Vietnam(Vn)*

Source: MIT Observatory of Economic Complexity (OEC)

As with Japan, signature of a FTA may be key to the UK's efforts to reverse its $2.6 billion trade deficit with South Korea, but that will still leave British exports far short of Germany's market penetration.

The UK's top 20 product group exports to South Korea address only 22% of the potential South Korean market and, stripping out the $2 billion of crude petroleum exported in 2017, the diminished total of UK export sales at $4.6 billion represent a less than 1% market share against Germany's 4.2%.

Note: In Appendix VI.2 product group exports from competing countries of $50 million or less are not registered.

HONG KONG
Appendix VIII.1 – Top 20 Import sources and export markets – 2017

Rank	Export market	$ billion	% of total	Rank	Import source	$ billion	% of total
1	China	16.40	12.0	1	China	256.0	42.0
2	Thailand	12.50	9.2	2	Singapore	60.8	10.0
3	Other Asia	12.00	8.8	3	Other Asia	40.8	6.7
4	India	10.30	7.6	4	South Korea	34.8	5.7
5	Vietnam	10.10	7.4	5	Japan	32.1	5.3
6	Switzerland	9.34	6.9	6	USA	30.5	5.0
7	UK	8.77	6.4	7	Philippines	14.8	2.4
8	Netherlands	6.14	4.5	8	Australia	14.2	2.3
9	UAE	6.04	4.4	9	Malaysia	13.6	2.2
10	Macau	5.42	4.0	10	India	12.7	2.1
11	US	4.08	3.0	11	Thailand	10.7	1.8
12	Singapore	3.67	2.7	12	UK	8.3	1.4
13	Malaysia	3.22	2.4	13	Vietnam	7.9	1.3
14	Philippines	2.99	2.2	14	Germany	7.8	1.3
15	South Korea	2.00	1.5	15	France	6.5	1.1
16	Indonesia	1.75	1.3	16	Italy	6.3	1.0
17	Germany	1.55	1.1	17	South Africa	4.0	0.7
18	Bangladesh	1.50	1.1	18	Belgium-Lux.	3.1	0.5
19	Japan	1.48	1.1	19	Indonesia	3.1	0.5
20	Israel	1.15	0.8	20	UAE	2.8	0.5
Sub-total		120.40	88.4			570.8	93.8
Hong Kong Total		$136 bn	100.0%			$609 bn	100.0%

Source: MIT Observatory of Economic Complexity

In 2017 the Hong Kong merchandise trade deficit of $473 bn was almost 3.5 times the level of exports. However, 92.7% of economic output is derived from the services sector, with Hong Kong as a leading global financial centre, having close links with the stock exchanges in Shanghai and Shenzhen. As a colony of the UK until 1997, Hong Kong operated as an entrepot for trade with China, but since the handover to China as a Special Autonomous Region (SAR) that role has dwindled. In 1997 some 50% of China's trading goods were transmitted through Hong Kong compared to 13% in 2015, as the mainland ports were opened up to international trade.

The top 20 destinations accounted for 88% of Hong Kong exports and the top 20 countries of origin for 94% of imports. Among the top 6 countries from which Hong Kong sourced products, imports greatly exceeded exports. Trade with the UK was almost in balance albeit at modest levels with exports at $8.8 billion and imports at $8.3 billion. Of the UK's main European competitors Germany, France, Italy and Belgium-Luxembourg were trading in surplus with Hong Kong, while the Netherlands was heavily in deficit.

Appendix VIII.2 – Top 20 products of more than $20 million imported by Hong Kong from the UK

Product	Import value $ billion	UK share exports (%)	Major Competitors Value of product imported ($bn)	All Total ($bn)
Gas turbines	1.58	19.0	Ch(1.0), US(0.9), Th(0.3), UAE(0.1, Du(0.1), Ja(0.1)	4.8
Gold	1.21	15.0	Au(11.0), He(0.9), US(3.4), Ja(2.6), Ch(5.2), Sa(1.8)	35.0
Platinum	1.07	13.0	SA(0.8), He(0.3), Ja(0.3), Ru(0.3), D(0.1)	2.9
Jewellery	0.58	7.0	Ch(3.0), In(2.1), US(1.7), It(0.7), UAE(0.7), Id(0.4)	12.3
Paintings	0.30	3.6	US(0.5), Fr(0.1)	1.2
Wine	0.21	2.6	Fr(0.5), Ch(0.4), US(0.1), Au(0.1), Si(0.1)	1.6
Cars	0.17	2.0	Ja(0.6), D(0.5), US(0.4), Ch(0.2), It(0.1), SK(0.1)	2.3
Measuring instruments	0.16	2.0	Ch(0.5), D(0.1), Ir(0.1), Ja(0.1), SK(0.1), OAS(0.1)	1.3
Antiques	0.15	1.8	US(0.2)	0.5
Broadcasting equipment	0.15	1.8	Ch(38.1), US(3.6), Th(0.7), Ja(0.5), Si(0.4), Ma(0.3)	45.4
Insulated wire	0.10	1.2	Ch(3.0), Ja(0.2), US(0.1), OAS(0.1), UAE(0.1)	3.8
Diamonds	0.09	1.0	In(9.1), US(2.4), BL(1.9), SA(0.3), An(0.2), HE(0.3)	15.4
Telephones	0.07	0.9	Ch(22.6), Ja(1.1), OAS(0.9), Th(0.7), US(0.5), Si(0.3)	28.1

(Continued)

Appendix VIII.2 – (Continued)

Product	Import value $ billion	UK share exports (%)	Major Competitors Value of product imported ($bn)	All Total ($bn)
Integrated circuits	0.07	0.8	Si(47.9), Ch(36.0), OAS(29.5), SK(21.8), Ph(9.8), Ma(8.3)	168.0
Office machine parts	0.06	0.7	Ch(17.7), Th(2.3), SK(1.7), Si(1.6), OAS(1.5), Ma(0.9)	28.6
Vehicle parts	0.05	0.6	Ch(02), Si(0.1), Ja(0.1), UAE(0.1), Si(0.1)	0.7
Chem. analysis inst.	0.04	0.4	Ch(0.4), US(0.3), Ja(0.2), D(0.1)	1.2
Thermostats	0.03	0.4	Ch(0.7)	0.9
Sculptures	0.03	0.4	US(0.1)	0.2
Aircraft parts	0.03	0.3	Ch(0.2), US(0.1), Fr(0.1), Ja(0.1)	0.6
Sub-total	64.15	74.5		346.8
TOTAL	$8.30 bn	100.0		$609 bn

Country key: *America(US), Australia(Aus), Austria(Au), Bahrein(BA), Benelux(BL), Canada(CA), Costa Rica(Cr), Czech Rep. (Cz), France(Fr), Germany(D), Hong Kong(HK), India(In), Iran(Irn), Indonesia(Id), Iraq(Irq), Rep. of Ireland(Ir), Italy(It), Japan(Ja), Kazakhstan(Kz), Libya(Li), Malaysia(Ma), Mexico(Me), Netherlands(NL), Nigeria(NI), Norway(No), Oman(Om), Other Asia (OAS), Philippines(Ph), Poland(Po), Qatar(Q), Russia(Ru), Saudi Arabia(Sau), Singapore(Si), Slovakia(Sl) South Korea(SK), South Africa(SA), Sweden(Sw), Switzerland(He), Thailand(Th), Turkey(Tu), United Arab Emirates(UAE), Unit,ed Kingdom (UK), Vietnam(Vn)*

Source: MIT Observatory of Economic Complexity (OEC)

Drilling down to the principal products that the UK exports to Hong Kong, Appendix VIII.2 identifies that the top 20 categories accounted for almost 75% of its trade in good, while the same categories represented 57% of Hong Kong's total import value.

Unsurprisingly, China was the lead supplier or the UK's main competitor in 11 product groups, with the US in pole position for only three low-value categories. Aside for cars (Germany), and wine and aircraft parts (France) the UK's major rivals do not feature as competitors. Therefore, the task for the UK is to rebuild its trading relationship with Hong Kong in the face of stiff Asia competition.

Note: In Appendix VI.2 product group exports from competing countries of $50 million or less are not registered.

CONTRIBUTORS' CONTACTS

Basck
Christian Bunke
Tel. +44 (0) 1223 654547
Email: christian@basck.com

British Exporters Association (BExA)
Michelle Treasure
+44 (0) 207 222 5419
Email: michelle.treasure@bexa.co.uk

Chartered Institute of Procurement and Supply (CIPS)
Trudy Salandiak
+44 (0) 1780 756977
Email: trudy.salandiak@cips.org

Coventry University
Dr Brian More
Tel. +44 (0) 7974 984928
email: BMore@cueltd.co.uk

Equipped 4 (IP) Limited
Dominic Schiller
Tel. +44 (0) 151 601 9477
Email: ds@equipped4.com

Harwell Science & Innovation Campus
Dr Barbara Ghinelli
Tel. +44 (0) 7500 106641
Email: barbara.ghinelli@stfc.ac.uk

ICC United Kingdom
Chris Southworth
Tel: +44 (0) 20 7838 9363
Email: csouthworth@iccwbo.uk

Legend Times Group
Tom Chalmers
Tel: +44 (0) 20 8127 0793
Email: tom.chalmers@legendtimesgroup.co.uk

May Figures Ltd
Dr Mark Graves
Tel. +44 (0) 1727 751080
Julia May
Tel. +44 (0) 1727 751080
Email: julia@mayfigures.co.uk

patentGate GmbH
Margit Hoehne
Tel: +49 (0) 3672 205 9962
Email: mh@patentgate.de

Olaf Swanzy
Tel:+44 (0) 7810 837479
Email: olaf.swanzy@pnoconsltants.com

RandDTax
Terry Toms
Tel. +44 (0) 1483 808301
Email: terrytoms@randdtax.co.uk

TIAO
Glynis Whiting
Tel: +32 (0) 495 56 17 17
Email: glynis.whiting@tiao.world

University of Buckingham Press
Jonathan Reuvid
Tel: +44 (0) 1295 738070
Email: jonathanreuvid@legendtimesgroup.co.uk